equal value

Carol S. Robb

Equal

An Ethical Approach to Economics and Sex

Beacon Press · Boston

Beacon Press
25 Beacon Street
Boston, Massachusetts 02108-2892

Beacon Press books
are published under the auspices of
the Unitarian Universalist Association of Congregations.

99 98 97 96 95   8 7 6 5 4 3 2 1

Composition by Wilsted & Taylor
Text design by Christopher Kuntze

LIBRARY OF CONGRESS CATALOGING-IN-PUBLICATION DATA
Robb, Carol S.
     Equal value : an ethical approach to economics and sex / Carol S. Robb.
        p.   cm.
     Includes bibliographical references and index.
     ISBN 0-8070-6504-8
     1. Women—Economic conditions.   2. Sex role—Economic aspects.   3. Social
justice.   4. Patriarchy.   5. Feminist ethics.   I. Title.
HQ1381.R63 1995
305.42—dc20   95-15090
                                                                          CIP

contents

acknowledgments

MORE THAN MOST, this book has emerged from work with many people, all collaborators. Funded by grants from the Association of Theological Schools and the Graduate Theological Union, I wrote chapters 1 through 5 on my sabbatical leave in 1989, and submitted them to groups of colleagues who, because of their teaching or professional expertise, were able to evaluate this work. Thus I thank Karen Lebacqz, Clare Fischer, Marty Stortz, Pamela Cooper-White, Lynn Rhodes, Jane Spahr, Coni Staff, Ellen Teninty, Kathy Johnson, Betty Pagett, Diane Deutsch, Jeanne Choy Tate, Lynn Jones, Rose Izzo, Mitzi Eilts, and Roma Guy for participating in wonderful daylong working sessions to improve the quality of the conceptualization, research, and writing that went into these chapters. I particularly thank Don Steele, Karin Case, Richard Randolph, Kathryn Poethig, and Fran Elton for the organizational and facilitation work that allowed me to listen to colleagues and students who provided valuable criticism of this work.

My colleagues at San Francisco Theological Seminary and others at the Graduate Theological Union have continued to help me understand the religious tradition out of which I write, and to show me how to put such understanding on paper. In this latter regard, Pat Lista-Mei has been absolutely central, and Mary Poletti, Dean Lewis Mudge, and the Faculty and Curriculum Committee of the Board of Trustees have supported me and spurred me on. Colleagues in Area II continue to add to my understanding of this work.

My editor, Susan Worst, has performed wonders in helping me shape complicated material, and I thank her for her brilliance.

Carol S. Robb
January 18, 1995
San Anselmo, California

chapter one

Introduction

T HIS IS A BOOK about sexuality, economics, and justice. In it I make the claim that women's experiences of sexuality compromise our access to the economy to an extent that is not true for men. I illustrate how this is so by describing how child-bearing and child rearing, domestic violence, sexual harassment, and lesbian identity affect women economically. (What I mean by "experiences of sexuality" is not only, or even mainly, confined to the realm of the erotic, but includes social pressures on women as sexual beings, and thus is related to a gender system.) Every woman will have experienced at least one of these compromises to her ability to take care of herself, and every man will be complicit in some way with the processes that compromise the security of women. This is because the economy is structured for men. I will argue that to the extent this is true the economy is unjust, and I will contribute to a conversation about what an economy that would not be unjust would look like. I will also draw some conclusions about what sexual ethics should look like in light of the intimate connection between gender, sexuality, and economics.

Suggestions for and about social change do not usually become full-blown and substantial until the conditions for such change are already present. In this case, there are women and men of good will who are already aware of inequalities in the work sphere and at home and are trying new patterns of relationship in both. Because the structures for work and for institutionalizing intimacy are slower to change than ideas about the need for change, people and the institutions we live and work within are experiencing stress. This stress reflects both a poor fit between people with new

ideas and institutions and people with older ones, and intraper-
sonal struggles, struggles within ourselves. Some of us consoli-
dated our identities and views of ourselves as masculine and feminine in one culture, a patriarchal culture, and are now trying to
behave in ways consistent with another culture, one that values
gender equality. It isn't always easy. Yet, as this book is being written, many of the conditions for gender justice are in place.

In this introductory chapter I will share some of the philosophical and biblical roots of our heritage regarding justice, since the
notion of justice is the main moral principle grounding this study.
The four chapters that make up the middle section of the book describe how women's access to the economy is compromised by our
experiences of sexuality. The concluding chapters will again take
up the question of what justice requires of us now, in light of this
exploration of women's experience, particularly as we might see it
affecting our notions of sexual ethics and economic ethics.

The Language of Justice

Justice is a primary principle for evaluating economic systems.
Today, many innovative scholars are constructing new theories of
justice, including John Rawls (*A Theory of Justice*), Michael Walzer (*Spheres of Justice*), Robert Nozick (*Anarchy, State, and Uto-
pia*), Susan Moller Okin (*Justice, Gender, and the Family*), Iris
Marion Young (*Justice and the Politics of Difference*), and Carol
C. Gould (*Rethinking Democracy*). If you read their books you
will discover that there is no consensus about how justice requires
us to change economic relations. Though I will not critique the
works of these scholars here, I use almost all of their theories in
some way, and the discussion that follows will not in any way dis-
place the importance of coming to terms with the ideas these authors propose.

Justice is defined by our philosophical forebears as giving to
each person her or his due. The problem is knowing what each
person is due. This problem is endemic to the purpose of ethics,
which is not founded upon uncontestable truths, but is rather the
process of trying to identify the best of several options, all or most

of which have merit. Doing ethics requires being engaged in a process of discernment which, if it is a responsible process, is always open to contention. Determining what people are justly owed has always been an important component of moral reflection.

As noted by Chaim Perelman in *The Idea of Justice and the Problem of Argument*, the language of justice contains different meanings, all if not most of which you and I use in our everyday conversation. These differences reflect the fact that there are several ways to discern what each person is due, and while they all seem more or less intuitively correct, they will conflict with one another when we try to honor all of them at the same time. As is the case in moral reflection generally, we need to decide what definition of justice should have primacy at any particular moment in history, with the understanding that at another moment another definition of justice should receive priority.[1]

For instance, justice requires that we treat all persons equally— justice as *equality*. If I am doing the same job and have the same job description as Alfred, it isn't fair for him to get a bigger paycheck than I do. We honor this definition of justice when we declare that there should be equal pay for equal work.

On the other hand, we also recognize that justice requires that people be treated in some way consistent with their *work*. If I worked overtime three days this week, I'll be offended if Alfred gets the same paycheck as I do when he didn't work *any* overtime and, in point of fact, left work early twice. In this way we use the notion that equal treatment can sometimes be unjust, particularly when people are not equally productive. This concept of justice is also operating when we notice that women's jobs are, and have been, different from men's jobs. While comparing different jobs is complicated, it is not impossible, and there are now modes of measuring job descriptions for *comparability*. By measuring such factors as skills required, danger level or discomfort involved, and responsibility for supervision over others, workplaces can be held accountable for justice by works in terms of comparable pay for comparable work. Pay equity efforts are geared toward achieving comparable pay for comparable work, and acknowledge that what people are owed is in many instances determined by the work they perform.

We also recognize the validity of justice according to *merit*. Merit refers to qualities that are less measurable than work performed, qualities that nevertheless make persons deserving. Product or result is likely to be measurable, but it is not all that is meritorious. We intuitively assent to the notion that those who try hard deserve recognition for their effort, even if, for reasons such as handicapping conditions, they do not produce commensurate with others. In addition to a person's or a group's effort, intent or desire often figures in assigning what is owed, as when a good faith effort goes wrong, or efforts to contribute to the social whole are undercut and blocked by discrimination and its historical consequences. Affirmative action laws in the United States, for example, are based on the notion of justice that involves merit. They recognize that members of groups discriminated against have to try harder than members of the dominant group to do anything, because of the prevailing headwinds of prejudice.

Of course, we also recognize that justice dictates that something is owed those who are in *need*. The need of others makes just claims on those who have more than enough for themselves. When people are not able to work, or to find work, we recognize the justice of providing a "safety net" to support those people until their situation improves. We may disagree on what constitutes eligibility for the safety net, but there is something of a consensus that need makes obligations on those not in need.

Justice according to *law* is a common definition of justice in U.S. society. People hire a lawyer and go to court if they think they have a case, regardless of whether they ought to press the matter in court in light of the other issues discussed here. Clearly, the law can be unjust, so it is the better part of wisdom not to overemphasize justice according to law in moral argument, but it is a reasonable expectation that a just society will protect all equally with the law.

Finally, there is the potentially galling notion of justice according to *rank*, that is, that you deserve according to what your rank in a hierarchy allots you. The military, some churches, and higher education still nurture this notion of justice, as do rewards based mainly on age. However, rank itself is usually justified by reference to past accomplishment or justice according to work, so it is rarely the only reason given for a particular allotment.

An economic system will be seen as just to the extent that it is perceived to honor appeals to conflicting claims *fairly*. We say an economic arrangement is *equitable* when a good-for-now compromise has been struck among parties arguing for conflicting aspects of justice. That compromise establishes which aspect of justice will have priority (for now), which has next priority, and so forth. Justice, fairness, and equity are therefore in practical terms interchangeable ideas.

Finally, one of the most frequent uses of justice language is in the appeal to human rights. A right is a just claim on others' treatment of you. By definition, a right cannot be unjust. Furthermore, because a society cannot guarantee its citizens a right to something it cannot provide, rights are historically defined. (We will consider human rights in more depth at the end of this chapter.)

Perelman's description of the meanings of justice brings to light the different ways we use the term and the fact that they all have a place but the priority of meanings will depend on historical circumstances and people's ability to make a case for one over another. In general terms, his treatment is a philosophical one, meaning not so much that philosophers created it (though they probably did) but that its justification is that people of good will who talk together can come to share this language about justice.

It takes no special revelation or other authority to see the usefulness of these ideas. We may disagree about which aspect of justice should receive priority, but the view that justice has at least these six different meanings, and that the meaning that should receive priority may change from period to period, can serve as the basis for a common language within societies or between societies, one that does not have to be justified by reference to religious authority or special knowledge. Because they focus on politics, class struggle, and interest group contention, political philosophers may not accept this view of justice, but they would propose another that also does not rely on religious truths or special knowledge as its justification.

John Rawls has another approach that could help us find a common language. He thinks the best definition of justice is that definition a group of people would come up with if they were sitting around a table talking to each other, without knowing the particulars about their own or the others' identities. If it were possible not to know your own social and economic status, gender, age, sexual orientation, race, or abilities, then your view of what is just could not be self-serving in these respects. Consequently, self-interest in defining justice would be neutralized. The principles that govern the distribution of harms and benefits in any particular society could then be arrived at by people who could imagine what it would be like to be in different people's shoes. Of course, in real life it is impossible to neutralize the bias that comes from social location, but what is important to Rawls is that a given set of principles of justice are correct only if they would be chosen by a group of people unfettered by the knowledge of how they would stand to lose or gain by such principles, who would therefore want to protect themselves in case they are, out from behind their hypothetical veil of ignorance, lacking status or special talents. I don't share Rawls's own formulation of the principles of justice that would be arrived at under these conditions, because I believe he does not value equality enough, but implicit in several of the chapters that follow is the notion that if men knew what it was like to be women, they wouldn't do the things they do or promote the programs they promote. I believe men's experience of male privilege prevents them from comprehending and being significantly affected by women's points of view.

Key to Perelman's treatment of justice is that the process of determining which criterion of justice to use in a given situation is one of contention—that is, of people articulating their points of view, listening to others articulate theirs, and attempting to win over people holding opposing views. Where imbalanced structures of power prevent people from articulating their views, or prevent others from taking those views seriously, a political struggle may be required to open the possibility of speaking and hearing.

Iris Marion Young and Robert Nozick might say that so far this treatment of justice has been primarily concerned with the distribution of social goods—income, status, leisure—and that's true. They would each recommend, for different reasons, that distributional views of justice need to be outweighed by other views.

Young recommends that we see justice as a matter of struggles against oppression, which may have distributional aspects but are not limited to issues of distribution of social goods. For her, injustice involves powerlessness, cultural erasure, and marginalization, and the injustice is not only in limits to the powers of consumption of certain groups, but also and perhaps more importantly in limits to their participation in the production of social goods. She argues that social justice is the capacity of a society to contain and support the institutions necessary for the realization of the values that make up the good life, and she sees these values as basically of two kinds—those that help citizens develop and exercise their capacities and express their experience, and those that support citizens' participation in determining their own actions and the conditions of their actions. Oppression and domination are institutional constraints on such self-determination.[2]

Young is of course correct; her argument reminds us that the *process* by which distributional matters get decided is also relevant, which is why the concept of due process has a venerable history in our understanding of justice. Honoring the process of participation does not supplant the need to discuss the principles of distribution, however.

Robert Nozick would also say that Perelman's view of justice over-emphasizes distributive issues, and that it ignores the rights that accrue to people by virtue of their producing social goods: if property is acquired by just (legal) means, then the products generated on or by that property justly belong to the property holder. Nozick so glibly collapses moral rights into legal rights that I have trouble using his perspective, but I agree with him (and with Young) that no discussion of justice that addresses issues of distribution alone can yield a well-rounded social program. Nevertheless, I believe the relationship between gender, sexuality, and economic distribution is a good place to begin.

Biblical Perspectives on Economic Justice

The treatment of justice as outlined above denies that there is any one criterion of justice that always trumps the others. If you are someone for whom the Hebrew Scriptures and the New Testament carry moral weight, however, there is an additional component in any discussion about what justice requires of us today. Specifically, because the Bible is an authority for Christians, Christians need to consider how the Bible treats justice, in addition to considering other authorities such as critical reasoning, the tradition of church teachings, contemporary experience, and the sciences. I write from within a tradition that holds the Bible as an important authority, and I believe that because the Hebrew Scriptures and the New Testament have been among the formative influences of all Western cultures, insights into biblical treatments of justice are relevant to us all in the United States.

It may come as a surprise that there is a program for economic justice in the biblical texts. Yet the Bible's economic ideas are a potentially useful resource, since it was written by people struggling to create new and better ways of life in the face of concentrations of economic and political power quite analogous to those of our own time. Of course, their vision was not always broad enough; these texts are marked by sexual, racial, and social stratifications that reflect rather than criticize the circumstances in which they were developed. Christians seek an emerging coherence from all the authorities, but at times such coherence is elusive, so moral maturity requires us to make conscious decisions about whether to adopt the principles and values represented in the texts by testing the truth of each in our own historical context.

In the Bible, justice is the main principle for evaluating the economy, law, and politics, but it is even more: it is the personality of God. Hence justice grounds theologically the sexual ethics I propose in Chapter 6, as well as the economic principles I propose in Chapter 7. That justice is my theological as well as philosophical grounding needs some comment. I mean by "theological justice" what I perceive to be a consensus among biblical scholars who see justice in terms of fidelity to the demands of a relationship. In short, justice is right relationship. The demands of a relationship are concrete and historical, and depend upon the nature of the relationship—whether between governance and citizenship, parent and child, teacher and student, or friends. Therefore, the requirements for a just relationship cannot be specified ahistorically or a priori. In this respect, biblical justice is similar to philosophical justice.

The righteous or just person as depicted in the Bible preserved the peace and wholeness of the community by fulfilling the demands of communal living. Historical, concrete situations of individuals in their communities—this is the context in which relationships make demands for rightness. Beyond the concern for the integrity of the person-in-the-community, however, justice is rooted in the nature of Yahweh as the defender of the oppressed. One cannot know Yahweh without defending the marginal groups in society. When they are exploited or forgotten, neither worship of God nor knowledge of God can result in true religion.[3]

I will trace how this notion of justice is embedded in biblical economic principles shortly, but here I call your attention to two theological ethicists who have explored biblical justice. For Beverly Harrison, justice is the heart of moral faithfulness and of our experience of God. It shapes the *telos*, the ultimate end, of a good community and serves as the animating passion of the moral life. Justice as rightly related community is the core theological metaphor of a Christian moral vision of life, according to Harrison, and, in addition, the attempt to discern what justice requires is the work of our common life, whether as citizens or as church people.[4]

Margaret Farley sees justice as a criterion by which we can know whether we should or should not maintain a specific commitment to love. Justice as the norm for a right love affirms the concrete reality of the beloved. We can fail to love at all the object in question. Or we can love with a mistaken love, affirming some aspect of the beloved's reality in a way that unintentionally distorts the whole or misses an important part of it. And we can love with a lying love, ignoring and distorting aspects of the reality of the one loved.

A love is right and good, however, when it aims to affirm truthfully the concrete reality of the beloved. In other words, love will be just when it does not destroy or falsify the reality of the person loved. A just love affirms the essential equality of persons, but it also attends to the differences among them in terms of capabilities and needs. It will take account of and respect the full autonomy of persons, and the meaning and value that they themselves give to their lives.[5]

Farley also explores the concept of covenant in Jewish and

Christian religions, noting the strengths, weaknesses, and perplexities of the covenantal traditions as a grounding for justice in personal commitments. Covenant, justice, and righteousness are interdependent norms in theological ethics. Justice is therefore theological as well as philosophical in nature, and it grounds sexual as well as economic ethics.[6]

THE HEBREW SCRIPTURES: LAND TENURE AND THE JUBILEE

The Hebrew Scriptures do not propose a specific economy because they take an agrarian economy for granted. They also assume an urban realm, but for the most part concern themselves with it chiefly to protect those in the agrarian economy from being destroyed by the military and merchant elites who live in the urban areas. The texts that contain specific principles for economic relationships—such as Leviticus 25, Deuteronomy 23, Nehemiah 5, Psalms 15, 37, 26, and 112, and Proverbs 19—are scattered throughout the Hebrew Bible, and were composed in different time periods. They contain principles that forbid interest on survival loans and the taking of debtors' necessities for life and livelihood as sureties for loans, as well as the humiliation of debtors or the violation of their homes; they provide for manumission of debt slaves on a seven-year cycle, for remission of debts and land foreclosed upon every seventh year, and for a return to the land every jubilee (or fiftieth) year.[7] In addition, these texts mandate a sabbatical year for the land, protective legislation for children, and a sabbath every seventh day for all, including slaves.[8]

These biblical strictures governing economic behavior appear to be focused first and foremost on the principle that large, extended family units (larger than a twentieth-century nuclear family), and the individuals in them, deserve protection from the tendency toward polarization of wealth and poverty. Since the primary way families supported themselves was by farming, they had to have access to land. Rather than using market forces to determine the distribution of land, their principle of distribution was one of rough equality, taking into consideration the geography and productivity of the land. (Some plots of land used for annual cultivation of cereals were probably distributed by lot at the village level, while land in intensive perennial cultivation was probably not distributed by lot because of the many years of care required to bring vines or olive trees into production.)[9]

As anyone familiar with farming knows, small landholders have cycles of feast and famine, and make it through the hard times by seeking short-term "survival" loans. Since small farmers have very little to offer for collateral other than their animals, their land, their children, or themselves, the consequences of defaulting on a loan are very serious. This was also true for the village peasants of the biblical world, and the overwhelming majority of references to debt in the Bible refer to such survival loans, not to loans of venture capital.[10] Regulation of these lending patterns was, then, an objective of some of the biblical economic principles.

The Canaanite economy, in which the Israelites were situated and against which they attempted to differentiate themselves, was marked by latifundialism, the tendency of wealthy landowners or merchants to accumulate land through what some would call the normal functioning of the market. They would make loans with high interest rates to small farmers, who, if they could not repay, would lose their land and their ability to support themselves except in a condition of servitude.

Canaanite landowners were not the only ones to engage in latifundialism in this region. As the Israelite state in Palestine became increasingly centralized under David and Solomon, the tendency of the ruling elites among the Israelites to accumulate land also increased. These elites favored importing luxury goods, to be paid for with the export of agricultural commodities, and they were able to control the state's taxation policies to convert subsistence and sustainable agricultural practices into a system of agriculture for export, often forcing risk-taking on the part of small landholders and then foreclosing on their land. The economic strictures set forth in the Hebrew scriptures criticized and put limits on this market-driven process: first, interest should not be charged on small loans; second, if farmers lost their land, it could be redeemed by relatives; and third, if there was no one who could redeem the land, the debt would nevertheless be canceled and the land returned to its original owner during the jubilee year, once every fifty years.

The institution of the jubilee limited the impact of poor luck or poor farming practices to one generation, preventing stratification from taking on a intergenerational quality that is much deeper and more rigid. The jubilee was a critique of the massive private accumulation of landed wealth, and of forms of large-scale collectivism that destroy any meaningful sense of personal ownership.[11] In this respect the economic principles in these biblical texts were rooted in agrarian kinship and village structures that favored the priorities of self-sufficiency and sustainability in subsistence agriculture, recognized the importance of retaining mutual risk-spreading measures, and valued rough social equality, or at least limitations on inequality.

Israelite society was conceived by the writers of these texts to be structurally dependent upon large family units that held land from which they could not be permanently alienated.[12] The theological justification for this was that the land belonged to God and the people on it were strangers and guests who were brought out of slavery from Egypt and given the land to use responsibly. Because it was God's land, landholders had responsibilities to the land, to wild creatures, to the poor, and to widows and orphans. Their private property rights to use the land existed within guidelines of obligations to others and to the land itself.

By building in a structural requirement that families be able to redeem land on behalf of relatives and have land returned to the family every fifty years, these guidelines recognized that family health depended in part on economic viability and that economic policies should protect the interest of the smaller kinship units within which individuals find their primary sense of identity.[13]

Israelite society was certainly not egalitarian, although the most disadvantaged, the social class of landless laborers, were given some protection by the prevailing economic practices. Most important of these was a sabbatical (seventh-year) release of workers who were slaves to landholders. This release did not result in their being returned to their own land, since they never had claims to land, but it did set limits on poor working conditions they may have suffered in any particular household, and "released" them to seek service in another household.

Israelite society was also profoundly unequal in that it was pa-

triarchal: women and children, along with slaves, were the property of the patriarch. The texts make it clear that the legal status
of women and children (as property) was mitigated by their social
status as members of families and human beings. But the economic principles of the Hebrew scriptures come out of a period
when women were conceived to have access to the economic realm
primarily through their husbands or fathers, and children only
through their fathers (which is why they recognize the economic
vulnerability of widows and orphans).

In our society today, even where the economy is still agrarian,
we do not view women and children as the property of male heads
of households, but that will indeed be their status if we do not
guarantee them complete access to the economy independent of
their relationship to a patriarch.

THE NEW TESTAMENT: JESUS' TEACHINGS AND THE *KOINONIA*

The scriptural warrant for undermining the patriarchal family
is clearest in the life and teachings of Jesus of Nazareth, and in the
practices of the Jesus movement and the very early Christian
movement.[14] It has been argued that Jesus was in many respects
antifamily because he was anti–patriarchal family.[15] However, he
did not thereby reject the leveling laws of sabbatical releases and
the jubilee. In fact, he is depicted as identifying his own ministry
as one of the proclaiming of a jubilee year (Luke 4:16–21). The
prayer he taught his disciples, known to most Christians as the
Lord's Prayer, is a jubilee prayer, asking for God to provide sufficiently during the fallowing of the fields and mandating the for-
giveness of debts. Jesus, and his movement as a Jewish renewal
movement, used the resources of Jewish scripture to extend the
principles of equality reflected in its debt easement laws to the
realm of the family.[16]

The world of first-century Judaism assumed that access to
property and economic relations in general was through the male
lineage. If a man died it was his brother's duty to marry his widow,
or she and her children would have no basis for a livelihood. Marriage was the main if not sole economic strategy for women. It
was, however, not organized in their favor. If a man suspected his

wife had been sexually involved with another he could divorce her, but a woman who believed her husband to be unfaithful had no such recourse. The asymmetry of property relations was reflected in the sexual realm.

Jesus seems to have had little interest in the goals of the family in his culture—the bearing of legitimate heirs or the acquisition, accumulation, and passing on of wealth. However, he preached a changed status for women by interpreting a passage of the creation story (Genesis 1:27) as an assertion that God created male *and* female in God's own image, to annul the rule attributed to Moses (Deuteronomy 24:1) by which a man might divorce if he found in his wife "anything improper." (One might say he used the Creator's actions to trump the Torah's later rulings.) He also used a second passage from the creation story (Genesis 2:24) to argue that the man and woman (or husband and wife) became "one flesh" in marriage. Jesus not only forbade a man to divorce his wife (Matthew 19:9), but also gave her a corresponding permanent and indissoluble claim on him as *her* sexual property. Henceforth, a husband's sexual freedom was to be no greater than that of a wife. The man and the woman were equals.

In addition to changing the status of wives, Jesus also altered that of children. Like women, children under twelve had no place in Temple observances and deferred to the head of the household's religious authority. When people brought children to Jesus for his blessing, his disciples tried to keep them away, reasoning that children were too insignificant to deserve his attention. Jesus, however, stopped them, saying, "Of such is the reign of the heavens" (Matthew 19:13–15). Another time, the disciples asked Jesus who would be the greatest in the reign of the heavens, and he placed a child before them and said, "Unless you turn and become like the children, you will never enter the reign of the heavens" (Matthew 18:1–4). One enters the reign of the heavens by "lowering oneself," giving up all claim to social status, security, and respect. As biblical scholar Elisabeth Schüssler Fiorenza puts it, "This saying is not an invitation to childlike innocence and naivete but a challenge to relinquish all claims of power and domination over others."[17]

The same principle stands behind Jesus' admonition to his followers not to accept such titles as "rabbi" or "teacher." "You are all brothers," he said. "Do not call anyone 'father' on earth, for you have one father—the one in the heavens"(Matthew 23:8–9). In the "new family" of Jesus' followers, there are only children, no patriarchs: the family structure of his age is completely overturned, and by negating the prevailing family structure, Jesus reversed the hierarchical assumptions that governed all of Palestinian life. [18] Even God, Jesus taught, was not so much the Father of the Universe but is running out to greet returning prodigals.[19] There is evidence in the Gospels that Jesus recognized that the economy as well as family structure was "engendered" to support patriarchal power, and that he made a deliberate effort to show a way of being together that was marked by economic and political relations of reciprocity and equality.

Jesus of Nazareth lived in a social structure marked by Roman imperialism and the increasing urbanization of Palestine. The first New Testament texts include more urbanites than the Hebrew Scriptures do, portraying Palestinian villagers, fishermen, and craftspeople as well as small farmers. And the letters of Paul and other missionaries reflect an urban experience—in Jerusalem, Corinth, Antioch, Ephesus, and other cities. The context of the inheritance of God's blessing and the goal of redemption as seen in Exodus and Leviticus, for instance, shifts to the *koinonia*, the "fellowship" of Christ, in the New Testament. Through this fellowship, Christians were promised the permanence, security, and inclusion that came from a tradition of assured access to land guaranteed by membership in the large families of Jewish society.[20]

The early Christian missionary movement used in its baptismal ritual the proclamation "There is neither Jew nor Greek, there is neither slave nor free, there is neither male nor female, for you are all one in Christ Jesus" (Galatians 3:28). This baptismal formula was a religious, social, and political statement about the equality of all who share in God's power. Jews, pagans, women, men, slaves, free poor, rich, those with high status and those with low status—all are without exception sisters and brothers.[21] In baptism, Christians entered into a kinship relationship with people coming from very different racial, cultural, and national backgrounds, and the house church community changed everyone's status. Jewish and Gentile women's status changed, since legal and cultural male privileges were no longer valid.[22] The status of slaves changed, since slavery was inconsistent with the "new creation" brought by baptism.[23] Christians' self-understanding as a new community was an alternative vision that clearly undermined both the Jewish and the Greco-Roman patriarchal orders.[24]

Paul had a role in furthering this egalitarianism in some instances and attempted to undermine it in others. On the one hand, he uses the full baptismal formula in his letter to the Galatians. On the other, he seems to have been disturbed by the independent authority the women in Corinth had discovered in the risen Christ, and for that reason he dropped the "neither male nor female" phrase of the confession in addressing them and argued with them to submit their prayer and prophesy (and perhaps also their teachings) to hierarchal structures marked by decency and order. However, it is clear in his first letter to the Corinthians that he didn't expect them to agree to his rationale.[25] According to Schüssler Fiorenza, "Gal 3:28 is a key expression, not of Pauline theology but of the theological self-understanding of the Christian missionary movement which had far-reaching historical impact."[26]

Through *koinonia*, the socioeconomic ethic of the jubilee tradition remained.[27] But can this concept bear the weight of an economic ethic to the degree that the jubilee and related provisions in Hebrew Scriptures do? One author claims yes:

> There is the same concern for the poor and needy (1 John 3:17), the same ideal of equality among God's people, both economically (2 Cor. 8:13–15) and socially (Jas. 2:1–7). There is even the same prophetic indignation at those whose sin deprives or defrauds fellow members of God's people of their rightful share in what God has given for the enjoyment of all people.[28]

Another author believes that the notion of God's people in the New Testament use of *koinonia* refers almost always to Christians alone. But I believe that this is due to the historical circumstances of the early churches rather than to the Greek concept itself. The Greek word *koinonia* and the concept to which it refers are not indigenous to Palestinian Judaism and do not appear in Jesus' teachings. But the concept had been known in Hellenistic Judaism, and Saul of Tarsus would have known the term. Seventy-five percent of the references to *koinonia* in the New Testament are found in Paul's letters.[29]

In Greek usage, *koinonia* could refer to all sorts of relationships, and frequently meant "having a share in something," and thus participation. It might also, though more rarely, mean "giving a share" of something, or imparting. It implied a common life and common good, which were related to justice, order, what is fitting or beneficial, and to friendship. It also implied a communal economy and equality, at least for citizens of a city-state, in contrast with private greed. Sharing together in peace, harmony, and care for others as part of humanity, even care for animals, constituted *koinonia* for the Greeks.[30]

In the New Testament, *koinonia* usually refers to the way Christians will respond to others because of having experienced fellowship with Christ; such actions would include support of missions, hospitality and benevolence, and financial sharing. The partners in such action are almost always Christians.[31] But keep in mind that Paul was addressing Christians who were organized into diverse "house churches," some of which were constituted by Jewish believers and some by Gentiles. There was no universal church, and often his concern was to get Christians to worship and work together in a single city. The service to all that is more typical of Greek usage of *koinonia* apparently took a back seat for Paul in the face of the lack of unity of the Christian churches. If we continue to limit the understanding of Christian *koinonia* to sharing with Christians only, the concept cannot serve as the basis for a socioeconomic ethic for us today. But to the extent that we lift our eyes from ecclesial concerns, we may be better able to experience the outward reaching to all of God's creation that comes from fellowship in God.

The egalitarianism of the Jesus movement and the early Christian missionary movement was normative for the household churches for most of the first century. The practice of coequal discipleship brought the Christian community into tension with its social environment, however, and particularly in letters to churches in Asia Minor, some missionaries, citing Paul or Peter as authorities, dealt with this tension by introducing the Greco-Roman patriarchal order of the house, or household code, into the house churches in the last decades of the first century.

Colossians, Ephesians, and the Pastoral Epistles (1 Timothy, 2 Timothy, and Titus) allow us to trace the beginnings of the patriarchalization not just of the Christian household but also of the church.[32] The Gospel of Mark (written at about the same time as Colossians) and the Gospel of John (written at about the same time as the Pastorals) repudiate the strategy of conforming Christian worship and social life to the patriarchal family, to structures of dominance and submission.[33] Mark and John appeal to Jesus himself to support their alternative stress on altruistic love and service. This evidence of the nonpatriarchal early Christian ethos allows us to see that patriarchal structures are not inherent in Christian revelation and community but instead permeated them slowly and with difficulty.[34] Then, as now, there was a tendency to establish community at the expense of the dignity of women, children, and slaves. The sacrifice of the egalitarian way of life may have allowed this particular political and religious perspective to survive, but I'm thankful that the egalitarian remnants of the Jewish, Jesus, and Christian traditions were not buried.

The six different meanings of justice presented at the beginning of this chapter are present in Hebrew Scriptures and the New Testament, and there is a priority given to some of them. In the Hebrew Scriptures, in the Jesus movement, and in the early Christian missionary movement before patriarchy was reestablished in the Asia Minor churches, *justice as equality* receives first priority. One of the main reasons for that priority is that it is necessary to meet human need. This is important. The commitment to equality in these scriptures does not appear to be premised on a five-year-old's concern that when one has more than another "that's not fair," though the five-year-old's insight has much to recommend it. Rather, the only way to prevent the growth of a sector of the population that persistently lacks sufficiency is to take measures to assure rough equality in the distribution of the means of production and of social goods.

What does this reading of the Bible mean for how we should do economic ethics today? Not that people seeking direction in the Bible should *mechanically* prioritize equality; sensitivity to context and attention to fittingness is wise for those who honor the texts, as it was for the people represented in them. But the Bible does favor a way of life, personal, political, economic, and religious, that measures goodness by the capacity to achieve mutual and reciprocal relationships among all.

Justice and Rights

One of the most common languages we use today in public discourse about justice is the language of human rights. There are two major views of what constitutes a human right, and a third view is now emerging that may prove more morally satisfying than the earlier two.

The "negative rights" perspective is associated historically with liberalism and is reflected in the Bill of Rights of the U.S. Constitution. Negative rights guarantee freedom from coercion and protection of due process. These rights are "negative" because they prevent others from interfering with one's efforts to construct a future of one's choice when that future is consistent with the freedom of other citizens to do likewise. The right to free political and religious expression and to due process are negative rights.[35]

The "positive rights" tradition contends that negative rights are almost meaningless unless people also have positive rights to food, clothing, medical care, education, and housing. Positive rights require outlays of social and economic goods, which might take the form of rights to work and to material security. Rights in this view are opportunities to participate in the benefits of social production.[36]

Conflicts about whether negative rights should take priority over positive rights reflect in part a disagreement about whether justice as determined by the law (as reflected in the negative rights tradition) should take priority over justice as defined by guarantees to basic necessities (or justice according to need). The United States, whose governing philosophy emerged from the negative rights tradition, has tended to favor the notion that a political community owes its citizens only the freedom to pursue their own definitions of their own good, although the view that basic needs create obligations on the social whole is embodied in federal programs (many now under attack) such as social security.

A third view of human rights is now emerging, one reflected in David Hollenbach's retrieval of the Roman Catholic human rights tradition and Beverly Harrison's feminist moral theory. In this view, a human right is a minimal condition or requirement for full participation in community with dignity and both negative and positive rights are necessary for the capacity to live in community with dignity.

One contribution of this emerging view is that it recognizes that communities have histories and that the requirements for participating in community with dignity may change over time. Exactly what fits the definition of human rights at any one time is a matter for public debate, with every corner of society heard from.

Since taxation is the primary means for redistribution of income in the United States and in market economies in general, discussion about appropriate tax policies is one arena where citizens' beliefs about rights and about justice become most apparent—as amply demonstrated by the current heated debates in congress. As I show how the U.S. economy is unjust for women, and also for many children, I will make some proposals that have tax policy implications and are therefore about distributive justice. My claims will not be limited to distributive justice arguments; some are more pertinent to visions of how production should take place, but I will seek to show that the language of distributive justice with which I began is useful for understanding the effects of the economy on women.

In my view, a priority on justice as equality and justice in the satisfaction of need emerge as the most demanding requirements for rectifying the injustices women currently experience. However, the injustices involved in the issues I describe are not limited to offences against equality and the satisfaction of need. Nearly every meaning of justice is offended as women attempt to care for themselves economically while in the process of bearing and raising children, dealing with sexual harassment and domestic violence, or accepting lesbian identity. In the course of making this argument, I will use the emerging theory that human rights must include both positive and negative rights, thereby verifying its relevance for issues of sexual ethics and economic ethics.

chapter two

Childbearing and Child Rearing

I BECAME PREGNANT under quite good circumstances, all things considered. My partner and I shared a commitment to having a child, I was in good health, and though we were in a new city with new, high-stress jobs, we had relative job security and relatively flexible schedules. We also had support from friends and colleagues, people who were wiser than we about what parenthood involves. The pregnancy was without complications, and our baby was born healthy and beautiful. But we were not prepared for the changes parenthood brought us.

Because I was new on the faculty, I was entitled to only six weeks paid sick leave. I cannot stress enough the supportive attitude of my colleagues and my partner's, but the seminary at which I taught had never had a pregnant faculty member before, and there were no structures for family leave. The federal government had not yet mandated family care leave, and even if it had, I would not have been able to afford a leave with no pay and no health care benefits.

I was particularly surprised at how deep the emotions linking me to this new baby were. He was six weeks old and just beginning to smile when I went back to bare-bones teaching, and I was neither physically nor emotionally ready to walk out the door to return to basic academic responsibilities. I felt then, as I do now, that I was robbed of time with my new baby—and of the time to heal and recover a sense of groundedness. Our son had to try to adapt to substitute care earlier than the fourth month recommended by pediatricians.

He was born in the middle of the academic semester, though, so my partner and I arranged our work hours so that I could return to teaching and yet limit substitute care to less than twenty hours a week. I taught in the morning, so my partner stayed with our baby when I was in class, then he went to work at noon and put in his eight hours. Two students helped in other time blocks so I could attend meetings and meet my other obligations; however, arranging our work in this way took some flexibility and cooperation from our respective work institutions—and it was not always easy. The good will and understanding were there, but we still had to get the papers graded or the job printed on time. We both had colleagues and customers or students whose own work could not be done without the part each of us had to play.

If under these relatively favorable work conditions we experienced a great deal of stress, how much more difficult must it be for those many, many women who have no maternity leave, no flexible schedules, no support from a partner or colleagues, no readily available substitute care, and no highly acclaimed neighborhood children's center to look forward to using when the child was two. This is the experience that physically linked me in a new way with millions of women and their children.

Among all the different ways in which pregnancy makes an impact on women and their partners (many of them wonderful), one which cannot be underestimated is the economic impact on the woman who brings a pregnancy to term and commits herself to parenting that child. Both pregnancy (whether or not carried to term) and child rearing (whether the child is one's biological child or not) affect women economically. Women become economically vulnerable through childbearing and child rearing, and employers treat all women differently than all men, as a pattern, because women could be mothers.[1] I argue that with respect to childbearing and child rearing, our economy offends justice with respect to work, equality, and need. This chapter then proposes that we, as a nation, should expect more of fathers in nurturing their children, and plan ways of supporting parents and their children through high-quality child care, parental leaves, substitute income, and flexible work arrangements while children are young.

Economic Factors and Consequences

Eighty-five percent of women in the United States will have at least one child.[2] All women who bear or adopt children become economically vulnerable to a certain extent. Men's life plans are also affected in a major way when a child is born, but in our society the mother of that child is likely to be affected economically to a degree that the father will not be.

EDUCATIONAL ACHIEVEMENT

Childbearing and the rearing of children make it very difficult for women to pursue education, and education has a direct relationship to economic standing.

In the case of a woman who has not yet graduated from high school, pregnancy and childbirth can make finishing high school difficult. Young women who allow others to adopt their babies still have the period of pregnancy and recovery to disrupt their education, and the length of that period is affected by whether the educational environment is supportive or punitive, by their own health during pregnancy, and by the availability of health care. The adoption process itself may weigh heavily on women who take that option, and while that concern need not necessarily prevent graduation, it can serve as a distraction or a depressant.

The decision to carry a pregnancy to term and parent the baby has even more profound economic effects. The younger a woman—or girl—is when she becomes pregnant, the less likely she is to complete her education. According to a California state task force on family policy, only 29 percent of those who become mothers at age fourteen or younger are likely to finish high school; the probability of graduation rises to 50 percent for adolescents who become mothers when they are seventeen.[3]

A high school diploma is crucial for even minimum economic well-being in our society. Fewer than half of white high school dropouts are employed and less than one-third of black dropouts have jobs. Workers without a high school diploma average only half the annual salary of those with college degrees, and they are five times as likely to be unemployed.[4]

When young women drop out of high school due to pregnancy and childbirth and decide not to marry as well, the economic consequences are doubly negative for the women and their children. Today we are witnessing a large increase in the proportion of births to adolescents who do not marry. The proportion of all such births to women twenty or younger who were born before 1945 was less than 20 percent, which still seems amazingly high given the stigma attached to such births. Since then, however, the proportion of births to unmarried women has steadily increased. Sixty-nine percent of births to women under twenty in 1991 were to unmarried women. This increase is due primarily to the increased proportion of white adolescents having intercourse at an early age, and the greater proportion not marrying before the birth of a child. The childbearing rate of black unwed adolescent women has not changed as significantly, even though an increased proportion have had intercourse, because of a decrease in rates of conception.[5]

For some young women who became pregnant at an early age, the decision to have a baby knowing there are few prospects for marriage may be an act of self-determination, a way of retaining some autonomy when marriage is seen to be the taking on of two children instead of one. Others choose to become parents when their partners would prefer abortion, and that decision may be a sign of their maturity and economic self-sufficiency.

In many cases, however, the decision of a very young woman to bear and raise a child is a result of her realistic calculation that mothering is her only future, even if it means economic stringency or even dependency. The decision not to marry and to seek public welfare may be a "rational" one, if the young woman and the child's father have little or no likelihood in the immediate future of having steady, family-supporting employment. This perception is particularly pervasive among young African-Americans, where the current rate of so-called illegitimacy is high (in 1991, 88 percent of all births to black women under the age of twenty were out of wedlock, compared to 59 percent among whites) not because young black women are conceiving more, but because they are marrying less.[6]

The consequences of the rise in births to unmarried adolescents are so seriously negative in the aggregate that the phenomenon as a whole should be seen as an indicator of a failure of right relations in our society. Those negative consequences include not only low educational attainment and low earnings, but also health problems for mothers and infants, welfare dependency, and child abuse and neglect. Adolescent childbearing is itself a predictor of a series of lifelong difficulties both for the mother and the child.[7] In addition, most teenage mothers are poor to start with, and receive poor quality education. Poor schooling restricts their job opportunities and reduces their incentives to delay childbearing. It takes a hope that education will bear fruit to sustain young women in their efforts to become educated. As it is, poverty is promoting teenage motherhood.

For older unmarried women, childbearing remains associated with extreme economic vulnerability, but black female-headed families are more likely to stay poor than white ones. Among unmarried mothers between the ages of twenty-five and forty-four, there is a 20-percent gap between black and white poverty rates.[8]

Because one out of two new marriages now ends in divorce, marriage alone is not a stable basis for economic security—education must be included in women's strategy for economic well-being. It bears mentioning that for women there is a strong correlation between obtaining higher levels of education and remaining single and childless during young adulthood. Higher educational levels are related to a later age of marriage for men also, although to a lesser degree, and the timing of marriage does not have as significant an effect on men's educational attainment.[9]

Women have completed high school in the same or greater numbers as men throughout this century, and since 1900 the average level of education for both men and women in the United States has gone up. But beginning in the 1940s and continuing through the 1960s, men's levels of education increased much more than women's, due to the advantage afforded men through the G. I. Bill after World War II. By 1984, women had returned to the same position relative to men that they had maintained during the first half of this century. The ratio of women to men college graduates now is .89.[10]

As we can see, childbearing and getting educated do not mix easily. Statistically, for every additional year of education that a U.S. woman achieves, she postpones her first child by approximately a year. I sympathize with the woman who, after graduating from high school in the northern midwest, going to college, getting in some master's degree work, and becoming a teacher in Boston, said the only way she escaped the fate of her classmates who are unhappily married with no prospects for economic independence was by keeping her legs together. It's a crude but graphic statement about the importance to women of delaying childbirth until they have the education they plan for themselves. Also graphic is the fact that only about 20 percent of women aged twenty-five to twenty-nine have graduated from college. Less than one-fifth of U.S. women have college diplomas (13.5 percent in 1993), and that is about the same percentage of the total population that has a college degree (14.5 percent).[11]

Of course, factors other than responsibility for raising children affect whether a woman will receive a college education. Class, gender, and racial prejudices, financial constraints, poor educational preparation, lack of academic interests or abilities, and other family obligations can all prevent a woman's attaining higher education. But, in addition, the impact of education on a woman's life plan is complicated by social and economic factors that may have as much an effect as education on women's economic standing.

SEX SEGREGATION AND THE WAGE GAP

Whether or not they are mothers, women are subject to discrimination in the labor force because they *can* be mothers. I will discuss two forms of such discrimination here. First, generally speaking, women are channeled into "women's jobs," a phenomenon known as the sex segregation of the labor force. This particularly affects women who do not have college degrees, but it has a bearing on the ability of almost all women to care for themselves and their children. Second, women's earning power is limited by the wage gap, the fact that men are paid more than women with comparable educational preparation, years in the labor force, and types of jobs.

Economist Barbara Bergmann, while combing the court records of pay equity cases, found that women are excluded by personnel policies from whole realms of job configurations in order to avoid mixing men and women where they must interact as equals, to avoid female supervisors for men, and to reserve training slots for male candidates for upper-level men's jobs.[12] In other words, job segregation reproduces in the paid labor force the subordination of women typical of the patriarchal family. When women are excluded from certain positions, either because men want to reserve the privileges of these jobs for themselves or because they don't want "no damn woman" telling them what to do, then women's participation in large sectors of the economy is precluded.

In 1985, 70 percent of all women employed full-time were working in occupations in which over three-quarters of the work force in question were female.[13] Female-dominated occupations and industries are the lowest paying. A recent study by the Bureau of Labor Statistics shows a strong inverse relationship between the percentage of an industry's work force that is female and the level of average hourly earnings in that industry.[14] Female-dominated occupations involve a lack of authority, vicarious rather than direct achievement, nurturant duties, and supervision by men.[15] Some "women's jobs," such as teaching and nursing, require college educations, so a college degree does not guarantee access to what have been men's jobs; however, without college educations women are more likely to be employed in sex-segregated occupations.

Between 1900 and 1970, occupational segregation by gender remained stable. Beginning in 1970, occupational sex segregation began to decline. The reason for this decline (a small one of about 6 percent between 1970 and 1980) is not primarily that men are moving into jobs women traditionally held, it is that women began to enter the traditionally male professional, technical, and managerial occupations. Most women still work in women's jobs, which are low-paying occupations, or are ghettoized within male-dominated professions, and they have less upward mobility than men, but a trend away from occupational sex segregation is emerging.[16] The question is whether the younger women in the labor force can maintain their less segregated positions. The young women of today may not be able to hold their positions in relation to their male colleagues when promotions and raises are distributed, in part because of what sociologist Arlie Hochschild calls the second shift—the disproportionate share of child rearing and homemaking responsibilities that women bear—which discourages them from competing for higher wages and promotions.[17]

Since the beginning of the century, more women are working in the paid labor force, for longer periods of time, and for more money than before. There is still a gender gap in wages, however. The ratio of female-to-male earnings remained consistently near 60 percent for full-time workers between 1900 and the mid-1980s. During the early 1990s the annual wage gap decreased, and women's annual earnings hovered around 70 percent of men's.[18] However, women's wages on average reach a peak at age forty to forty-four, when they are about the same as those of male workers starting out at age twenty-five to twenty-nine.

Younger women are closing the gap at a much faster rate than older women, primarily because of their higher educational levels. (In 1991 the ratio of annual earnings for full-time women workers relative to men in the same age group were 79.5 percent for ages twenty-five to thirty-four, 68 percent for ages thirty-five to forty-four, and 60 percent for ages forty-five to fifty-four.)[19] However, the gender earnings gap persists and cannot be accounted for by objective factors—work interruptions, educational differences, and differences in experience—alone. Together these factors account for only about five percentage points.[20] Access to education and work experience alone will therefore not eliminate the pay gap for U.S. women. Gender and racial discrimination in all its blatant and subtle forms continues. At every educational level, men earn more than women.

Median Annual Earnings of Women and Men for Full-Time, Year-Round Workers by Educational Level, 1991

	High school	College (B.A.)	Masters
White			
Women	$18,252	$27,840	$33,604
Men	26,790	40,624	46,978
Black			
Women	16,957	26,333	30,988
Men	20,731	31,032	40,815
Hispanic (of any race)			
Women	17,179	25,669	———
Men	21,690	32,972	37,832
All			
Women	18,042	27,654	33,122
Men	26,218	39,894	40,002

SOURCE: Institute for Women's Policy Research briefing paper "The Wage Gap: Women's and Men's Earnings," 1992, which uses statistics from the U.S. Department of Labor, Bureau of Labor Statistics.

Partly for this reason, divorce in the United States has a harder economic impact on women than men, and in fact usually benefits men financially. Because married-couple families have two potential adult earners, and because the husband is likely to have higher earnings than the wife, families headed by women alone are likely to be poorer than married-couple families. When marriages end, as they do 50 percent of the time, the poverty rate for women goes up, while men's economic standing usually improves.[21] One reason for this disparity is that women typically receive custody of the children after a divorce, and more than two-thirds of mothers of children from an absent father receive either no child support or less than the agreed-upon amount.[22] This situation creates a double bind for women who are the sole heads of families: the need to work to support the children and the inability to take many of the jobs available because they cannot afford trustworthy child care.[23]

It's worth noting that improving the ability of women workers to organize and bargain collectively is a significant component of a strategy to improve women's wages. Union membership or coverage by a union contract more than doubles white, black, and Hispanic women's odds of earning above a minimum sufficiency wage.[24]

Women in the United States, like men, work primarily for economic reasons. Forty-three percent of the women in the labor force are single, divorced, separated, or widowed; another 25 percent are married to men earning quite modest incomes, and the earnings of married women who work is 44 percent of their husbands' income.[25] The cultural expectation that women will find their main fulfillment in child rearing is internalized across class, and one effect of this expectation is to discourage us from competing harder for our share of what we have produced, or can produce; another effect is that employers view women as less attached to the labor force than male employees and take our claims to advancement and pay less seriously than men's.

Occupational segregation is an offense against justice according to equality insofar as it channels women and men into different jobs on the basis of gender when gender is irrelevant to the skills necessary to do a given job. The wage gap is an offense against justice according to work since the work women perform is remunerated less than the work men perform, not because our work is inherently or objectively less productive, but simply because it is performed by women.

CHILD CARE AND SOCIETY

Because our society fails to spread the costs of child rearing, women, one by one, pay the costs. And yet the well-being of its children is a major indicator of whether a society has a secure future. No one segment of our society—women—should be disproportionately responsible for the costs of the whole society's project.

One indicator of the general presumption that child rearing is a private matter is government policy regarding childbearing. Roberta Spalter-Roth and Heidi Hartmann, two economists from the Institute for Women's Policy Research, have tracked the effect of childbirth and maternity leave policies on women's earnings. They document the ways in which women bear a disproportionate share of the cost of childbirth because the nation does not have a wage replacement maternity or parental leave policy.

Comparing women who have babies in a particular year with women who do not, Spalter-Roth and Hartmann found that white women's economic circumstances, measured in terms of earnings alone, are negatively affected in the year they give birth, and more dramatically in the next two years. White new mothers' wage rates dropped, and simultaneously their hours of housework and their receipt of public assistance increased. Black women earn less than white women in the year before birth and in the birth year, but in the two years following the birth year their earnings are higher than white women's, because more black new mothers move into the labor force. For all women, the earnings lost because of childbirth total $31 billion annually.[26]

The Pregnancy Discrimination Act of 1978 was the first federal policy to limit employers' rights to fire women when they become pregnant, and it was also the first to require employers to provide the same disability insurance or other benefits for childbirth as they do for illness. However, this federal policy was not comprehensive, because it allowed individual employers to determine what kind of disability leave policy they would provide.

The next advance came in 1993, when Congress passed the Family and Medical Leave Act. That legislation guarantees the jobs of workers who request up to four months of leave in a two-year period for medical reasons, including childbirth, or to care for a dependent, but these leaves need not be paid leaves and the legislation covers only employers with fifty or more workers.

Even this limited, unpaid leave was gained only after much debate. In 1989, when Congress discussed the feasibility of requiring employers to provide job protection to workers who must take unpaid family leave, the U.S. Chamber of Commerce adamantly opposed such legislation. It said the cost to employers would approximate $16.2 billion a year in a "worst-case scenario" (100 percent of the work force covered, both parents, for eighteen weeks following childbirth and for five days to attend to sick children each year). It conceded that this estimate was high, and then lowered its estimate for more moderate use of coverage to $2.6 billion. However, the General Accounting Office (GAO), assuming 75 percent of the work force in businesses with more than fifteen workers, would use the leave, one parent at a time, using twelve weeks for a new child, estimated the cost at only $500 million.[27]

Businesses were not eager to hire a replacement for a worker on leave, train him or her, and contribute to unemployment benefits for the replacement when the permanent worker returned. Representatives from corporations that already had parental leave policies in place countered that employers who accommodate the needs and concerns of new parents are repaid by higher productivity, less employee absenteeism and illness, increased length of time on the job, and faster return to work. The GAO took a similar position.[28]

The discussion of costs to employers is relevant to moral reflection on the value of parental leaves, but without recognizing the extent to which women workers bear these costs now the calculations are incomplete. Considering the Spalter-Roth and Hartmann estimate that women as a group lose $31 billion in earnings annually in order to give birth, even the worst-case estimate of the Chamber of Commerce does not come near sharing in the cost of the new generation.

I do not believe that business should shoulder the whole cost of parental leave; however, all of society has a stake in a healthy start for little citizens, not women workers alone, and that cost should be shared more equitably than it is now.

THE UNDERVALUATION OF CHILD CARE AS A VOCATION

Women (and men) who are full-time parents and homemakers pay spiritual as well as economic costs. Because their work is not valued as real work by their peers who enter the paid labor force, they lose self-worth. If a parent chooses to make at-home work and full-time parenting her (or his) vocation, this vocation should be celebrated for the contribution it makes to the community, many of whose institutions, such as schools, religious organizations, libraries, and hospitals, depend upon someone being "at home" to volunteer for support work.

Besides unpaid but crucial labor in such settings, at-home parents provide continuity of care and intimate knowledge of children's development patterns, in their own homes and in the neighborhood. Now that more mothers are in the paid labor force than not, the mothers (primarily) who are *not* in the paid labor force often become the unofficial care givers of the neighborhood—a mixed blessing. On the one hand, they may prefer their children to play with friends at home so they have confidence they are not getting into mischief, or worse; on the other hand, it becomes next to impossible to have private time with one's own children, to supervise their chores and homework, when numerous friends have congregated. This is also a justice issue, particularly when parents in the paid labor force presume that at-home parents—mostly mothers—will fill in the gaps, not only for unscheduled time, but for school outings and related responsibilities. On what basis can we build just community relations if we undervalue work in the home yet depend on it?

This undervaluation of parental work in the home is reflected in the market's treatment of child care workers out of the home. According to 1987 Census Bureau figures, child care workers—teachers and aides—earned an average of $9,952 a year. Their turnover rate is 35 percent annually (conservatively) and the average length of stay in a job is 2.7 years. (The average U.S. worker in all occupational categories stays in a job for 6.6 years, so the turnover rate of child care workers' is much higher than average.) If we want a stable environment for our children, one in which they can form relationships upon which to build trust, then we will have to increase salaries and provide benefits commensurate to the professionalism required to provide that environment.

Clearly, the devaluation of child care as a vocation offends justice according to work, yet since it is difficult to measure the "outputs" of child care, it may be more accurate to see this offense as one which fails to give to each as she merits—and as a reflection that ours has become a society that places a low value on everything that cannot be measured and then sold.

Raising the Next Generation: Public Policy Implications

I have outlined five ways in which women currently pay a heavier share of the cost than do men for accomplishing the care and nurture of the next generation: education becomes more difficult for women than for men with children; in the labor force, sex segregation and the wage gap limit women's earning power and give a premium to maleness; women give up earning power when they raise children, because there are few if any structures to broaden the sharing of the cost of lost wages; in the event of divorce, men often do not pay their fair share of child support; and child care as a vocation is undervalued. According to the principles of justice we have discussed, women should have equal access to education, jobs, and salaries, even though our differences from men with respect to our childbearing capacity require that additional social supports for child rearing be put in place to make such equal access possible.

Far from being an abstract and distant procedure, the search for justice requires that we understand the concrete details of the lives of persons who are affected by social policies already adopted and those being considered for the future.[29]

PROCREATIVE CHOICE

Childbearing is only one out of many possible sources of self-esteem and social location for women who bear children. Relationships with partners, friends, and extended family, education, employment, community service, and time for oneself also constitute strong pulls on women's identities, so that the timing of childbirth is of utmost importance, as is our control over that timing.

The greater the availability of effective methods of birth control, the more motherhood can be an identity to be chosen after reflection. Access to reliable birth control is the first, essential condition that makes it possible for women to choose life plans autonomously, that is, without coercion, in accord with values we as moral agents hold to be true and consistent for a moral community and a just society.[30]

The ability of women to plan their futures and develop aspects of themselves other than parenting skills depends in part on continuing access to safe and legal abortion. The Centers for Disease Control calculated that among the 1.36 million abortions performed in 1987 (constituting about 30 percent of all pregnancies in this period), 72.8 percent were for patients who were unmarried. In a smaller sampling of this population, three-quarters of these women said that having a baby would interfere with work, school, or other responsibilities, and half said they would like to have children in the future.[31]

Women who obtain abortions are predominantly young, white, unmarried, and childless. Among married women, black women are about two-and-a-half times as likely as white women to have abortions. According to children's advocate Marian Wright Edelman,

> Having a child can mean a substantial loss of family
> income to a married black woman. Among two-parent
> families with incomes over $25,000, 83 percent of black
> women work, compared to 62 percent of white women.
> And the black woman's salary contributes a bigger share
> of total family income than does the white woman's.
> For many married black women, an additional child may
> tip the scales back toward economic insecurity.[32]

However, procreative choice is not only about limiting our childbearing, it is also about nurturing and protecting those children we do parent. In order to make a real choice to bear children, we also need access to good medical care before and after delivery, good health care for our children, a place to live with them that is safe and allows comfort, and nutritious food. These are material conditions that together support those who make a commitment to the future by having children. In this sense, procreative choice involves much more than a guarantee of privacy in matters relating to our reproductive selves. Rather, we as a society will have to undergird those supports that are required by the recognition of procreative choice as a right.

This is not to say that rights to reproductive choice should not be accompanied by responsibilities. All citizens, and particularly those who decide to reproduce, should be responsible for learning about their bodies and their sexuality, and that information should be made available in the usual educational channels. We all should be responsible for living our lives in such a way as to avoid endangering the unborn as well as our children, and we should have the assurance that food and drink procured through the normal channels will be wholesome. We should be responsible for planning our work lives so that children can have their needs met, including their need for time and nurturance from us, and, concurrently, we should have access to employment that gives us the means to necessities without having to sacrifice home life. We should each be responsible for considering the well-being of other species when we contemplate having a child, and concurrently know that our jobs and purchases are organized sustainably. Our individual capacities to live out our responsibilities are deeply affected by the social structures we live in, and as individuals we are not capable of controlling all the factors that impinge upon family lives. This is why family policies at all levels of government should be evaluated in light of a commitment to women, children, and the community—and why procreative choice should undergird such policies.

FAMILY POLICIES

Failure to develop family policies offends justice in that it deprives women of what we need to participate in the community with dignity. We need such policies to make it possible to choose life plans without coercion, in accord with values we hold to be true and consistent for a moral community and a just society.

Economic justice for women requires the nation to make a commitment to government policies that support families, in the form of high-quality child care (including day care centers), maternity and parenting leaves with wage replacement, and flex-time in the paid labor force. These benefits should be funded in such a way that families who cannot afford them can receive them anyway, while families who can afford them contribute to their cost.

As a nation, we have the resources to support these policies. One possible means of providing income support during family leave is by extending temporary disability insurance (TDI) as it currently exists in five states to all other states, and expanding it to cover serious family emergencies and new-baby leaves. In states with TDI (California, Hawaii, New Jersey, New York, and Rhode Island, and also Puerto Rico), because even employers with very few workers are covered, more employees are eligible for paid leave than are eligible for unpaid leave under federal family and medical leave legislation. Further, a majority of those benefiting from TDI are women, in part because TDI provides paid leave for the period of incapacitation due to pregnancy. Temporary disability insurance is funded when employees and/or their employers pay a small percentage of the employee's salary into an insurance fund. In return, employees are provided leave with replacement of their wages in the event they become seriously ill.[33]

Other family policies focus on greater support for child care outside the home. I am convinced that this issue hinges on political will rather than on availability of resources.[34] Evidence from nations in Europe, cited by Sheila Kamerman and Alfred Kahn in a major study of child care policy, indicates that this is the case.[35] Germany, Hungary, Sweden, and France have policies to attenuate the negative effects of childbirth on the mother's health, in addition to her loss of income, but the United States does not. All the countries studied provide cash and in-kind income supports for child rearing, except the United States. All countries studied, except the United States, provide a benefit that assures income replacement, totally or in large part, for the loss of earnings by women at the time of childbirth and for some time immediately thereafter. This benefit is wage-related and covers about 90 percent of wages, and the costs fall not on industry but on the society at large. The amount of time covered by this benefit ranges from three and a half to nine months. The Swedish benefit is an entitlement to both parents. This benefit is seen as a form of short-term insurance, covering one year at the most.

In some countries, these benefits were intended to increase fertility, but no industrialized country has successfully increased fertility over an extended period of time. Sweden is the only one of these countries to make an explicit commitment to equality between men and women, and learned on the basis of other attempts at family policy that parental benefits restricted to women function to reinforce traditional roles for women and to keep women in an inferior position in society. As the example of Sweden indicates, when men have a right to parental benefits and take them, job discrimination against women decreases.

To promote gender equality, benefits designed to replace or substitute for earned income must be earnings-related rather than flat-rate. If benefits reflect previous wages, even if there is a ceiling, there is more incentive for men to participate in responsibilities relating to early childhood care. The disparity between benefits given to rich and poor, a main concern of those who support flat-rate benefits, can be reduced somewhat by progressive taxation.

Every country studied, except the United States, has a policy about how to develop and provide care arrangements for children under the age of three. In the United States, parents must enter the market and find service in regulated or unregulated family day care homes, in social agencies, in centers sponsored by religious organizations, or in centers operated by the profit sector. Only the United States relies on day care centers for children over three, views day care and preschool as two separate systems serving the same age cohort, and is not committed formally to covering all children through one standard system.[36]

How do the countries that have such child care policies for very young children finance them? Societies that want to offer care are able to do it by combining national, state, and local subsidies with parent fees.[37] And the fact that citizens in the United States do not currently pay for such subsidies does not mean that people without young children pay no costs. Failure to be intentional about child care has effects on children and families, effects which in turn affect the whole society, and these must be considered and weighed in the balance.

These effects include poor quality of out-of-home care due to a lack of standards or a failure to enforce them; the development of stratification in child care services when market forces are the main mechanisms for developing them; pressures to reinforce a traditional family style, whereby women either stay in the home and thus are limited in their earning capacity or bear the private stress of managing both child care and paid work; and the creation of a poorly paid class of women who care for the children of those women who go into better-paid arenas of the economy.[38] In short, at stake is economic justice for women and a nurturing environment for our children. These are high stakes.

But improving the quantity and quality of out-of-home care for children is not enough. We must also create more ways that mothers and fathers can stay with their young children. Paid parental leaves with job security and proportional benefits for part-time workers are two such possibilities, but many small businesses would not be able to extend benefits like these and survive. It is therefore government's responsibility to help with these costs.

With respect to developing better and more comprehensive child care services, I would appeal to the principle of subsidiarity, a Roman Catholic social principle stipulating that social issues should be handled at the lowest (that is, the most local) level of society where they can be handled effectively, thus maintaining responsibility as close as possible to the affected citizens. I would claim that parents and school districts have to be involved with the issues of early childhood care, and municipal and state support is also needed. Employer-sponsored child care is available to employees of some corporations, offering relief as well as risk to some families, the risk being that if the institution fails both the job and the child care will be lost. Private enterprise may have a major responsibility in the provision of child care, but only when the provider is accountable to standards derived from independent agencies informed about what constitutes high-quality child care. The national government should have responsibility for child care as a national priority, unifying and buttressing state standards, and perhaps providing some subsidy to local and state agencies. This is the lesson I derive from looking at other industrialized nations, who, like the United States, have experienced a significant shift of women from the household economy to the paid labor force.

In short, the concern that it would be too costly to provide the social supports for high-quality child care is a legitimate concern, but we have good evidence that we can responsibly design such supports and afford them. Failure to do so, under these circumstances, is an offense against our collective responsibility to address a social need by bringing to bear resources at all levels of our common life—the family, neighborhood, city or town, county, region, state, and nation. In this respect, justice requires we give what is due according to need.

WHAT ABOUT THE CHILDREN?

In rights language, no one has a right to anything if it is inconsistent with justice for all people. That is, social support for high-quality child care cannot be a right if it wrongs other groups—such as children. Are children wronged by out-of-home child care? Most children have working mothers, and most will in the future.[39] This means that many children are receiving substitute or supplemental care, and we should know whether that care is beneficial or harmful.

Substitute care for children three years and above is not the major part of our worry, since even in the United States we have had relatively long experience with preschool nurseries and we know that there are ways to ensure our children's well-being in these situations. However, we need to know more about the effects of infant and toddler day care.

As a result of their investigation of the effects of child care services on children under three, Kamerman and Kahn reached several conclusions: Little is known about the consequences for very young children in placement in family day care (in a home with a care giver who supervises a small number of children), the major form of day care for under-threes in several countries. By its nature, family day care is difficult to supervise, and quality varies greatly from poor to excellent. Regarding center care, much more can be said. There are no known negative consequences of "reasonably decent" group care, where physical setting, ratio of care givers to children, and preparation of care givers is appropriate. Indeed, there is some evidence that some children do benefit from group care.[40]

For instance, the New York City Infant Day Care Study, a longitudinal study, compared low-income children reared at home, children with center experience, and those in family day care. Final measurements took place at age three. On all measures of intellectual, social, and emotional functioning, children attending infant day care programs for several years did as well or better than equivalent samples of home-reared children. The families (parents and siblings) using infant day care programs did not appear to be greatly affected by these programs. No relationship emerged between the child's age at entry and his or her psychological development at thirty-six months. In this study, the major difference observed between group and family programs related to nutrition and health care rather than to psychological development (the group programs provided higher-quality food and health services). The two types of programs were found to be basically equivalent in their effects on the children's psychological development. It could be that group programs enhanced intellectual performance, and that family programs positively affected social competence—but the case is not conclusive.[41]

Research efforts since the beginning of the 1980s have helped us understand that multiple variables affect children's intellectual, social, and emotional well-being. It is not enough to ask about the effect of day care alone on young children. We must also be sensitive to the possible influences of social class, gender, family organization, the role of parents, and the personality of the child. Consensus about the neutral effect of out-of-home child care is fragile, largely due to some continuing doubts about the long-term effects of such care on infants and the concern that the bulk of child care provided outside the home is not of the high quality required.

The major way researchers test the impact of day care on the social and emotional development of infants is through "attachment" studies. It appears that babies become attached to their parents more strongly than to anyone else in a large variety of caregiving environments, cross-culturally, and that this attachment usually occurs during the second half of the first year of life. Studies using a technique of measuring attachment, when they are methodologically rigorous, do find evidence of some disturbed parent-child attachments for 47 percent of infants who are in full-time day care (defined as more than twenty hours a week) starting before the infant's first birthday. Substitute care for more than twenty hours per week takes a toll on almost half the infants involved in terms of attachment to their mothers. Boys seem to be more affected than girls, and when mothers are employed full-time, attachment to fathers is also threatened. However, it helps infants' relationships with both mothers and fathers when a father, rather than a center or other substitute care giver, provides the care.[42]

Other factors that influence the quality of attachment include the personality of the infant and the degree of family stress. When there is a high level of stress (caused by divorce, unemployment, or poverty, for instance), parents are not as emotionally available to the infant, and infants who were secure at one time can become insecure at a later point. On the other hand, infants can also move from being anxious or insecure to being secure when environmental factors change.

Given a relatively unstressed family situation in which the primary care giver is emotionally available to the infant on a consistent basis, daily separations of a limited duration do not appear to seriously affect the quality of attachment. However, according to at least one research summary, the best predictor of later pathology in children is a cumulative frequency of stressful life events coupled with an insecure attachment in infancy.[43]

The effects of extensive infant day care must be followed very closely in the coming years. This research has been marked by methodological difficulties, and consensus is fragile.[44] Meanwhile, the policy implications of these findings seem to point consistently in these directions:

As a nation we need to take seriously the need for high-quality infant day care. High-quality care includes a highly involved staff, a low infant-to-care-giver ratio (three to one or four to one), small group size (eight to twelve for infants, and twelve for toddlers), stability among care givers, and care giver competence. These conditions are expensive; good infant day care is costly. So is poor infant day care, however, and as a society surely we would rather pay the first price than the second.

A major justice issue in child care is the way we treat child care workers. It would not be a sign of a just society to re-create a stigmatized, low-paid role for working women in which they now do for low pay and for other people's children what most women previously did for no pay but for their own children. In such a situation, care givers would be carrying the major burden of decent-quality child care. To avoid exploiting others, we must secure adequate public subsidy and mandated minimum pay standards, and recognize that they will constitute a major expense.[45]

Alternatives to infant day care should be available to working parents who would prefer to be with their babies during the first years of life. Minimally, we should be able to guarantee paid parental leave for four to six months.[46] In addition, we should not stint in our efforts to shorten work weeks and devise phase-in schedules in order to support parents who balance child care and work, so that children do not have more than twenty hours per week of substitute care. This may require a kind of social insurance to provide family allowances for income replacement.

Fathers should have equal responsibility for seeking adjustable work weeks. There is a good possibility that child care will remain undervalued as work as long as it is seen as "women's work."

In conclusion, we must not treat lightly the care of our youngest ones. Whether our infants are cared for in their homes by one or more parents, in another home, or in a group care situation, the younger the child the more carefully we should handle and nurture them. In an overall context of commitment to the well-being of our children, we can devise group care and perhaps family care situations that can substitute for some parental care. But they require high-quality environments, competent care givers, and a low ratio of care givers to children—all of which are costly. With this kind of commitment, we will not do an injustice to our children when we seek economic justice.

CHILD CARE AND POVERTY

The percentage of the U.S. population that is poor declined dramatically during the 1960s, changed little during the 1970s, and then began rising in the early 1980s. Using the official definition of poverty, the percentage of the population in poverty was 22.2 in 1960, 12.6 in 1970, 13.5 in 1987, and 14.5 in 1992.[47] The last figure represents 35.7 million people, and it does not include the homeless.

In order to understand who is in poverty in this nation, we need to explore the feminization of poverty. As a group, the poor have come to depend more on women as breadwinners, yet the gender gap in wages handicaps these women's efforts. The growth in the proportion of poor families headed by women, among blacks and whites alike, has resulted from several demographic factors, notably a sharp increase in the incidence of divorce and separation, an increase in independent living by unmarried mothers, and a decline in poverty rates for "male-present" households and the households of the elderly.[48]

Universal access to high-quality child care, then, is key in addressing the structural components of poverty. A few statistics underscore the importance of child care to the women who are heads of households: the poverty rate for single mothers with earnings is about one-third of that for women with no earnings; the poverty rate for single mothers of children under age six, when the women worked full-time all year, was one-tenth that of nonworking mothers; the main reason nonworking mothers in poverty give for not being in the labor force is child care responsibilities and the lack of adequate and affordable child care services.[49]

In this era of constant pressure for welfare reform, it may be important to recognize that 40 percent of Aid to Families with Dependent Children (AFDC) recipients already work. They do not generally have steady full-time employment, reflecting the volatility of the low-wage labor market, and they earn only about $4.29 an hour. Therefore, to limit AFDC benefits to two years (as some propose) would only contribute to the economic instability of these families, because even if they worked full-time, year-round at the jobs they hold, these women would generally not be able to bring their families above the poverty level through their work alone. One would wish that as much effort would be expended developing a full-employment policy as is expended now on welfare reform.[50]

An important piece of this picture is that poverty is not something that always persists across time for a given individual. Persistent poverty is the experience of only a small portion of the people exposed to poverty (10–11 percent). Poverty is not necessarily something passed from one generation to the next, either;

the more likely outcome for a child reared in poverty is for that child to move out of poverty as an adult.[51] Antipoverty programs *are* effective in helping families move out of poverty—when they are designed to do so. Support for child care is an antipoverty program.

Poverty among young mothers has been a particularly intractable problem. As mentioned above, whether black or white, young women under the age of twenty-five who head families are very likely to be poor. Yet when teenage mothers have free access to high-quality day care for their children, particularly day care with an appropriate educational component, they have an increased likelihood of completing high school, getting postsecondary training, and becoming self-supporting. The children of teenagers benefit from high-quality day care also, as is reflected in the mental test scores of these children. Easy access to good day care service beginning in a child's infancy is a source of developmental support for both teenage mothers and their children.[52]

The demographic shift toward single-parent families in all social strata has been well documented.[53] (Women are the sole breadwinners in one-fourth to one-third of the families in the world, so this phenomenon is not limited to the United States.)[54] This shift in household structure has lowered mean incomes for all families, especially those of African-Americans. Other economic factors are multiplying the risk women and children are facing. There is a growing inequality of income among our nation's families. In the early 1990s, the richest one-fifth of families had ten times the income of the poorest one-fifth, as compared to a six-to-one income ratio in 1967. Wages and salaries for low- and middle-income workers have been stagnant, while wages and salaries at the upper end of the scale have risen.[55]

As a nation, we have given the largest political voice to an economic strategy that proposes to address poverty through a "trickle-down" effect from economic growth. Yet we have not insisted that our nation plan our economic growth in such a way as to benefit the poor—which is why economic growth since the early 1980s has benefited the wealthy at the expense of the poor. Proponents of "small government" contend that we cannot use macroeconomic strategies to address social problems, but they have used such strategies to benefit their own. This is an area for which we as a nation have moral responsibility to provide new direction.

The Long View

Every moral argument takes place in a context that has a history. The history relevant to this argument concerns the changes in family structure that have occurred concurrent with changes in the economy in the United States since colonialization. The economy was household-based in colonial times.[56] Every member of a household contributed—even children, to the extent their age allowed—in agriculture, the making of cloth and clothing, preserving food, selling or exchanging the products of the household. Children were workers and didn't have a protected "childhood" as we know it today. Generally speaking, the more children in the family, the more stable was the family support system.

During the nineteenth century, with industrialization, the economy became characterized by separate sexual spheres. Commodity production left the household, as did men who went to work outside the home, leaving women's work in the home. The economic value of children declined because they were excluded from the paid labor force, at least after legislation to protect them from exploitation was passed. Concurrently, average family size decreased.

We are in a period of moving away from a separate-sexual-spheres economy to one in which men and women participate equally in the paid labor force. Women have eroded the separate-spheres economy by moving into it, and the economy is changing from one that depended primarily on "men's" jobs, one based on manufacturing, to one in which the new jobs created are primarily "women's" jobs, related to the service sector. Women were pulled into the paid labor force in part, and in part we walked of our own accord, attracted to the financial independence that paid work promises. In 1950, 28 percent of all women were in the paid labor force; by 1993 the figure was 57 percent (72 percent for men). The major impact of the transformation of the household has been on married women with children. While in 1950 about 24 percent of married women with children were in the paid labor force, by 1993 that figure had risen to 72 percent.[57]

All children have fathers, yet fathers have not moved to take responsibility for child care and housework to a degree equivalent to that with which women have moved into the rest of the economy. On the whole, fathers have not experienced the kind of qualitative shift in their identities and responsibilities that mothers have.[58] And the economy, specifically the organization of paid labor, is still structured to complement earlier patterns of family life, though now it cannot bear the weight of that form of social organization. Increasingly, there is no one at home to attend to the vital tasks that were accomplished by the unpaid labor of women during the era of industrialization.

While people have made adjustments, some positive, some negative, to the new situation of the majority of mothers working, the stresses and strains experienced in families, particularly with regard to child care, are viewed as private matters to be solved in individual ways. As a nation, we have not yet grasped child care as an issue that has a bearing on the common good to the extent that we must take collective responsibility for formulating family policies that support workers who are also parents. At stake is the possibility of economic justice for women, justice for our children, and wholeness for men.

THE CHURCH'S TASK

Religious organizations—from the Catholic church to mosques to synagogues—are already active in the child care arena. In fact, "the church" (meaning Christian churches of all denominations) is the largest single landlord for day care programs in the nation.[59] By general standards, religious-housed programs in child care measure up rather well. True, programs developed by these organizations tend to run larger group sizes than for-profit programs housed in their buildings. And staff members of child care programs are not considered employees of the religious organization, even when the program is operated wholly by the congregation, and therefore they do not ordinarily receive health care benefits or pensions provided by national religious agencies. These latter aspects of child care programs supported by religious groups should be criticized and monitored. But the overall quality of their programs for children is something of which these groups can be proud.

As I see it, Christian churches in particular have another arena of responsibility: to reconstruct theological perspectives with respect to the value of women and what we have considered women's work. The image that emerges as I reflect on the enormity of this theological task is one of women baking bread, whether at home or in the back of the bakery, and men breaking the bread before the congregation. As women who were once excluded from ordination move into the professional ministry, we struggle with the cultic requirement in the "mainline" denominations that only the ordained can break the bread baked by homemakers and workers. After all, the liturgy of the Eucharist remembers the Passover meal of Jesus and those who participated in his new way of radical egalitarianism.

In the process of revaluing women and women's work, the church must be willing to encounter several layers of what I see as idolatry which are nearly impervious to criticism. The first layer is the assumption that the common good is constituted by the aggregate of individual goods, defined by each individual independently. In contrast, a biblically based economic ethic would witness that the material conditions necessary for participation in community with dignity are binding on the whole community, and have priority over other goods, particularly on the freedom to enjoy luxuries. In effect, the first theological task is to disentangle church thinking about justice from its assumption that the sole content of the meaning of justice is freedom. Freedom is a high value, and will be a mark of a just economy, but only in relation to a higher value—the just response to need.

Another layer of idolatry within the church is the assumption that sexuality is dirty by virtue of our embodiedness, thus if we are going to have sexual pleasure we should pay for it. Sex negativity is directly related to society's abdication of collective responsibility for child rearing: "You played around. You got pregnant. Now you deal with it." This same attitude buttresses many anti-choice perspectives, and it is no accident that many people who are opposed to the licensing of churches for child care, guaranteeing standards for the stability and safety of care, are also opposed to procreative choice with regard to abortion. The church has an immense theological task in disentangling sexuality from our notions of sin, and it is a task that is fundamental to revaluing women and our work.

Sexual Harassment

I WAS ONLY MILDLY interested in sex roles as a component of discrimination until I began reading about sexual harassment of women in the labor force. Until then, I had seen traditional sex roles as simply a reflection of nonreciprocal power among women and men: although they reinforce and perpetuate relations of unequal power, I thought, they do not cause relations of domination.

My study of sexual harassment has not caused me to abandon this view altogether, but I now believe that confronting traditional sex roles is a very important piece of envisioning and creating a just economy for women. Women's effectiveness in the workplace is severely limited by sexual harassment, yet harassing behaviors are difficult to challenge because frequently the offended person, the offender, and their coworkers view those behaviors as normal or routine. It is time to appreciate the extent to which sexual harassment is rooted in social and personal expectations about how women should behave in relation to men, because these expectations make it harder for women to succeed at work, stay in their jobs, and earn as much money as men.

The Sexual Significance of Work

Work in the paid labor force is a way of earning a living and a component of the life project for most women and men, but work can also be an arena for sexualized conflict. Work and professional success are loaded with sexual meaning, and that meaning tends to be different for men and women because of the different socialization of males and females.[1]

For many men, success at work is very important because their work is central to their identity as males. Work status and pay are seen as measures of a man's power, dominance, and ability to compete. On the job, disagreements about specific tasks or policies can take on great significance for men because they see or feel their masculinity to be at stake. When women and men work together, it is possible for a man to "lose to a woman," inevitably more shattering to a male's self-image than to be bested by another male.[2] No wonder there is so much irrational resistance to women in jobs that were once held solely by men.

Women also have an emotional or psychological stake in doing well at work, but in a far more complex way. Although many women feel that their success in the work sphere is important not only for themselves and the well-being of their families, but also because *all* women are on the line (particularly when the job is one not traditionally held by women), female socialization is intrinsically incompatible with behaviors that are associated with success in most professions. Women are socialized toward passivity, nurturance, deference, acting emotionally, and relating well to others. Expressing competence usually requires self-assurance and willingness to argue a point against a colleague or a superior, and hence it is not uncommon for women to feel like they have to choose between "being competent" and "being feminine." Male socialization conflates competence and masculinity, while in female socialization there is a conflict between them.[3]

Some women resolve this dilemma by becoming "Iron Maidens" who suppress their expressions of warmth or sensitivity in order to be recognized as competent workers, but to do so they must cut off an important way of moral knowing. Those who suppress their emotions change their personalities, not only at work but in every other arena, for who we are in one part of our lives inevitably affects how we act in others. This behavior also reinforces an organizational ethos that communicates that whole people are not relevant to the work at hand. Nevertheless, the role of Iron Maiden is perceived by many women to be the best of a set of bad solutions.

Alternatively, women can deal with male-female tension in the workplace by forming a bond with one particular man. David Bradford, Alice Sargent, and Melinda Sprague describe four types of dysfunctional male-female roles they have found in work situations, all of which undermine a woman's ability to express competence and in this respect have a limiting effect on her access to economic goods.[4] These role pairs are of course not inevitable for male/female interaction in the workplace, but they occur frequently enough to warrant a look. They exist because they resolve, albeit in an unsatisfactory way, the sexual tensions men and women experience in working together. These reciprocal roles may not be assumed consciously, and their power in part lies in their commonness in daily interaction. Rooted in masculine and feminine stereotypes, these roles limit the range of behavior of both men and women, rather than encouraging them to respond appropriately to the situation; they are powerful because they serve certain needs the players may have, whether acknowledged or not.[5]

The first role pair in the Bradford, Sargent, and Sprague scheme is the "Macho" and the "Seductress." Both of these roles are heavily sexual, whether or not sexual acts take place. The macho man wants the woman to be impressed with his male potency, and he relates to her in terms of her physical attractiveness, while putting down her competence in other areas. The Seductress needs to have her sexual attractiveness affirmed, and her potential availability serves as a source of power, for she confers an aura of potency on the men she chooses. The cost she pays is that she is seen more as a sexual object than as a capable coworker. In addition, since being attractive is her first priority, she may not be as competent a worker as she could be.

The "Chivalrous Knight" and the "Helpless Maiden" are another role pair. He sees himself as strong, competent, and responsible for the protection of women. He is respectful of women, but does not expect much from them, and consequently does not give them the same responsibilities and tasks he would assign to men. The Maiden takes advantage of the Knight's protectiveness, playing helpless and asking him for help in problem solving. In serving her, he may become angry because he is being used, but to challenge the game the Knight would have to acknowledge the Maiden's competence. The cost to the woman in this role pair is that she does not learn to solve the problems on her own.

The "Protective Father" and the "Pet" role pair often occurs between an older man and a younger woman. He is again the protector and she again a dependent, but she is not as likely to be manipulative as the Helpless Maiden. Her role is to cheer on her Father, laugh at his jokes, encourage him to talk about himself, and refrain from contributing her own ideas or challenging his. The Pet is not seen as available sexually, as the Seductress is, but the cost is similar: her femininity is validated at the cost of being able to express her competence directly.

The "Tough Warrior" and the "Nurturant Mother" pairs a man who suppresses all emotions and communicates self-sufficiency with a woman in whom he can confide. He is very good at competition, independence, and giving ideas; he lacks the ability to collaborate, relate interdependently, and receive ideas and help—except from a Mother. The Nurturant Mother is not perceived as a potential sexual partner, but rather as a confidante to whom others turn for support. She is seen as wise, sensitive, able to understand men's predicaments. The costs to her are that she loses the ability to take independent initiative when to do so would challenge the men to whom she gives support. Her critical abilities are limited, and she tends to shield men from accepting responsibility for their failures or their current tasks. Furthermore, the role confirms the stereotype that men are rational and logical, while women are emotional.

Bradford, Sargent, and Sprague call our attention to role patterns that men and women often fall into as ways of coping with the tensions of working together. I would add the role pair of the " 'Feminist' Man" and the "Sexualized Colleague."[6] She is competent and enjoys her capabilities, and her expression of power in the work arena is generally positive. He is attracted to her because she is capable, and he sees himself as a progressive man who enjoys women as equals, yet instead of working with her solely as a colleague, he pursues her as a lover. If she becomes his lover, he uses that arena to undermine her in the work area. Familiarity in the relationship outside work compromises the energy and impetus for a dynamic relationship at work. She pays the cost again, as the arena in which she expressed her competence directly is now complicated with concerns to mute her capabilities when they come into conflict with his.

In all these instances, the women's role is dysfunctional for success in the work arena. Men are also limited by these roles, but mostly in ways that enhance their feelings of competence.

Each of these roles distorts a strength into a weakness. The ability to ask for help is not, in general terms, a character defect; it is an acknowledgement of our interdependence with other people. However, it becomes a problem if, as in the case of the Helpless Maiden, it becomes a (conscious or unconscious) manipulative strategy to exert control over other people. The ability to listen and empathize is invaluable; it is one source of our moral imagination and absolutely necessary for communication, parenting, and friendship. But nurturance and listening become problematic when they deflect us from appropriate and independent action, as they do for the Nurturant Mother and the Pet. Relationships need to be mutual if they are not to be exploitive. When physical attractiveness becomes more important than anything else, as it seems to be for the Seductress, this devalues other aspects of ourselves that deserve more acknowledgment, use, and affirmation. Role pairs like these are noxious for both men and women in that they split up by gender values and characteristics that should not be divided, and this imbalance prevents attitudes and behaviors appropriate to the situation.

These workplace roles reveal the subtle mechanisms—with which women often cooperate—by which women are prevented from exercising the leadership and control of which we are capable. These control mechanisms are not just silly, they are vicious. And when these subtle mechanisms do not work to maintain male dominance in the workplace, there are others, perhaps equally subtle.

For example, researcher N. M. Henley found that touching helps maintain dominance of white over black, old over young (until a certain age, after which it is young over old), wealthy over poor, and male over female: the one who initiates touching presumes access to the other's body. There are other such power displays: people in the dominant group demand and receive more personal space, more control of time, more territory, more respectful forms of address. They make more jokes at others' expense, practice less self-disclosure, make more interruptions of others, speak more, have more control of conversation topics, get more relaxation, make greater use of gesture, tilt their heads and smile less, and avert their eyes less.[7]

These power displays are stereotypical characteristics of male behavior. If women use them also, they are very likely to be considered deviant by their peer group, and if a woman does not respond to group pressure to fall back into "role" she may be isolated, even by other women.[8]

What Sexual Harassment Is

Sexual harassment has a long tradition in this nation. The sexual exploitation of enslaved black women is an early, extreme, and brutal form of sexual harassment, representing the far end of the continuum of abuses that have been labeled as such. But sexual harassment did not have a name until 1975, when the phrase was first used to name phenomena that women experienced at work.[9] Since that time, the Supreme Court has found that sexual harassment is a form of sex discrimination, and as such is against the law, specifically Section 703 of Title VII of the 1964 Civil Rights Act. Employers are now responsible for communicating to all employees that sexual harassment will not be tolerated in their organizations, to help set the climate of safety and security for all workers.

In addition, the notion that sexual harassment is solely a phenomenon of the workplace is changing. We now recognize that harassment can occur at home, at church, on the phone, at school, in the psychiatrist's office, on the street. It may be that sexual harassment is an inevitable product of the patriarchal family structure in which fathers/husbands control economic goods and the mothers/wives provide nurture and service. When women attempt to play any other role, in any sphere of social life, men may try to put them back "in their place" with the use of sexual harassment.[10] Since the focus of this chapter is the way sexual harassment contributes to women's economic vulnerability, the workplace will receive more attention here than other social spheres, although the status of women in one social sphere is connected to their status in others.

There are three main forms of sexual harassment. One is "quid pro quo" harassment, typified when a boss says, "Sleep with me or you're fired, demoted, or do not get the promotion." An illustration of this pattern is the case of Adrienne Tomkins (*Tomkins v. Public Service Electric and Gas Co.*, 1977). Tomkins, a stenographer for a large utility, asked her boss for a promotion. He asked her to lunch to discuss the matter, but, at a restaurant in a local Holiday Inn, refused to discuss the promotion at all; instead, he pressed her to check into a room with him. She left him, went back to work, and complained to other company officials. She was demoted and eventually fired.[11]

Quid pro quo episodes typically begin when the boss acts amorously, expressing his affection or attraction. (The boss is usually but not always male in these situations.) This behavior is indistinguishable from other kinds of courtship until it is refused. Then the boss retaliates, using his position at work to get back at the woman for refusing to go along with him.[12]

Another type of sexual harassment is "atmosphere" harassment. In this pattern, the harassing behavior is hostile, intimidating, and taunting, rather than sexually inviting. An illustration of this pattern is the case of Debby Ukarish (*Ukarish v. Magnesium Elektron, Inc.*, 1981), the first woman to do production work in a rural chemical manufacturing plant. The coworker to whom she was assigned to be trained for more difficult work was a man who had already made hostile remarks to her ("Do you want this rod up your cunt?" "Do you want a belly full?"). Instead of training her, he left her alone to do dangerous work without instruction, and one day he not only taunted her but provoked a scuffle. Ukarish was fired; her coworker was not.[13]

In atmosphere harassment, several men often participate in the hostile behavior; typically they are coworkers rather than superiors, although superiors may condone their behavior. Atmosphere harassment is more likely to happen to a woman who is in an occupation in which men predominate, while the quid pro quo pattern usually happens to women in traditionally female occupations. Atmosphere harassment can take the form of sexual slurs and jokes, sexual graffiti, and posting of sexual pictures, but from the outset there is no mistaking the hostility motivating the pattern.[14]

A third pattern of sexual harassment is called contrapower harassment, which occurs when the person targeted has formal power over the abuser. The abuser often retains anonymity, so the targeted person has no way to punish these acts or keep them from recurring. An example might be the harassment of women professors by their male students; when a professor goes into the lecture hall and finds a message on the blackboard suggesting she would enjoy an act of sexual violence of a lethal nature, or a student writes a message on an evaluation form that he is sexually frustrated and would like to make love to her, contrapower harassment has occurred.[15] The effects of contrapower harassment are similar to "power-down" and peer harassment: they contest the woman's authority and stature and may interfere with her work, they may undermine her feelings of integrity and confidence, they may make her afraid to work at the office in the evenings or on weekends.

Peggy Crull, research director of the Working Women's Institute, postulates that there is a continuum of harassment situations, depending on the extent to which the harasser has economic power over the harassed.

> At one end of the continuum are behaviors that appear to have as their goal some sexual / social interaction and at the other end hostile, threatening, and degrading acts that seem to serve as a substitute for patriarchal power. Corresponding to the sexual / social end of the continuum are situations where the harasser holds the greatest amount of economic power over the woman and where the sex-typing of the jobs are the greatest. Corresponding to the hostile end of the continuum are situations in which the man has

the least amount of power over the woman and where she
is violating patriarchal norms of the work place by holding
a male sex-typed job.[16]

It is crucial to understand that sexual harassment is affected by
how much power the men have in relation to the women. In the
traditionally female occupations that have males in the role of superiors, a male boss has the direct power to hire and fire. As in the
traditional home, he has economic control over the "wife," who
provides nurture and services, and, as if he were in the home,
he wants to treat his female subordinate as a wife because he
consciously or unconsciously believes that her job carries that
implication.

In traditionally male occupations, the female coworker is
threatening a sphere of power over which men have had control.
The men are her peers and without the direct power to hire and
fire. They can only make life miserable for her in an arena that may
well be the only arena where they feel they have any power at all.
From their perspective, she is out of her rightful place; in intimidating and humiliating her, they are trying to put her "back in her
place," where she is to do supportive, wifely work—certainly she
is not to compete with them or to achieve a modicum of economic
power.

While these prototypes are poles on a continuum, many cases
of sexual harassment reflect a power relation somewhere in between. For example, if a waitress harassed by customers who pat
and grab, make sexual comments, and leer does not respond, or
responds negatively, the customers have no direct economic power
over her except that of withholding tips, but they may also complain to the waitress's boss.

Dynamics in combination with sexism may be involved in sexual harassment cases. For example, some male-faculty / female-
student harassment incidents can be viewed as compensatory ges-
tures made by faculty who have experienced an erosion of the
prestige of their profession; they use their power over students to
gain back some lost prestige and consider access to female students to be a perk due them.[17]

Or consider the example of one woman who worked for years

with a man who never gave her any affirmation for her work; he was routinely critical, gave credit to others for her accomplishments, and bypassed her for promotions. He did not have the direct power to hire or fire her, but he had the power to make her life miserable because she was, in his perspective, out of her place.[18] A court decision in *Lipsett v. University of Puerto Rico* concurs that such hostile behavior is sexual harassment. The court found that even where certain statements are not explicitly sexual, they are still forms of sexual harassment insofar as they are charged with antifemale animus.[19]

Though women have the experience much more often than men, anyone may be a target of harassment. Among men who report being harassed, the vast majority describe the encounter as male-initiated.[20] But certain categories of people seem to be targeted more often than others. According to researcher Donald Maypole, those categories are:

- the young,
- the unmarried,
- the highly educated,
- members of a racial or ethnic minority (particularly if male),
- those who hold trainee positions (or office / clerical positions, if male),
- those who hold nontraditional positions for their sex (e.g., female law enforcement officers, male secretaries),
- those who have an immediate supervisor of the opposite sex,
- those who have an immediate work group composed predominantly of the opposite sex.[21]

On the basis of several discussions of sexual harassment in the literature, I would add to the list gay men and lesbians.[22] Among women, lesbians are affected particularly sharply by sexual harassment. Some of the men who harass them cannot fathom that women can achieve identity and intimacy independent of men, and are so threatened by such independence that they will threaten or even sexually assault a lesbian woman to "bring her in line." Lesbians may also be more aware of sexual harassment because they are not seeking sexual intimacy with men at all.[23]

DEFINING HARASSMENT

Sexual harassment is defined by the 1980 guidelines of the Equal Employment Opportunity Commission (EEOC) in this way:

> Harassment on the basis of sex is a violation of Sec. 703 Title VII. Unwelcome sexual advances, requests for sexual favors, and other verbal or physical conduct of a sexual nature constitute sexual harassment when (1) submission to such conduct is made either explicitly or implicitly a term or condition of an individual's employment, (2) submission to or rejection of such conduct by an individual is used as the basis for employment decision affecting such individual, or (3) such conduct has the purpose or effect of unreasonably interfering with an individual's work performance or creating an intimidating, hostile, or offensive working environment.[24]

Under these guidelines, employers are responsible for the conduct of their supervisors, agents, employees, and others toward their employees. That responsibility exists even if a supervisor's actions were contrary to the employer's policy and the organization did not know, or could not reasonably be expected to know, of the supervisor's behavior. Furthermore, if any individual is treated with favoritism as a result of sexual favors granted, other employees can be considered to have experienced sex discrimination.[25]

Behaviors that characterize sexual harassment include verbal abuse; subtle pressure for sexual activity; sexual remarks regarding clothing, body, or love life; touching, patting, or pinching; leering; brushing against the body; overt demands for sexual activity; physical assault.[26] In fact, the EEOC has determined that constant referral to women as "girls" is sufficient for a reasonable cause determination that Title VII has been violated.[27]

Often it is only when a woman hears that verbal abuse is one form of sexual harassment that she can make sense out of an extremely negative work situation she's experienced or is experiencing. Until then, she may have assumed that the tension between herself and men at work was personal, caused by her words or actions. The rubric of sexual harassment helps women understand when the abuse is directed toward them as *women*, because of their gender.

The EEOC's definition of sexual harassment is written in gender-neutral language, though the preponderance by far of harassing incidents are initiated by men. The EEOC acknowledges that sexual harassment has an economic dimension—that women's jobs, promotions, and other work conditions may well be at risk—but the definition's gender-neutral language, though appropriate for public policy, obfuscates the fact that sexual harassment is usually intended to curtail women's access to the economy.

Another definition, suggested by Edward Lafontaine and Leslie Tredeau, acknowledges male cultural privilege over economic goods and women's bodies: "Sexual harassment is defined as any action occurring within the workplace whereby women are treated as objects of the male sexual prerogative."[28]

The male prerogative allows men to impose sexual requirements in the context of unequal power, it has been structurally guaranteed by women's dependence on men for their material survival, and it has led to the condition in which women are socialized to assess their personal worth in terms of their desirability to men.[29] Men exercise sexual prerogative by retaliating against women who refuse sexual access. Men who have no direct power to hire or fire can also exercise sexual prerogative by claiming the work site as their turf; if they keep women economically dependent, they will have sexual access to women—not necessarily their coworkers, of course, but women in general. In both instances, men are acting on a basic assumption that they have a right to have their sexual needs or desires met *because* they are men, and that women have a basic obligation to satisfy men's sexual needs or desires, providing nurturance, a feeling of power, or even sport.

When women harass men, the male prerogative may not seem to apply, yet in many cases it does. One clergyman described a situation wherein a woman asked to see him to discuss theological matters; she arrived dressed very provocatively and made it very clear to him that she was open to a sexual relationship with him.[30] A male colleague remembers an incident when he was teaching in a small college; a woman student made an appointment to see him, at which time she offered to have sex with him in return for an A. He felt the proposal came totally out of the blue—there was nothing in their prior relationship that prepared him for any relationship with her outside that of faculty member and student.

In both these instances the male sexual prerogative remains intact. The woman is harassing *up*, initiating what she perceives to be a bargain in which she will gain some benefit from the male's use of his power. In these cases, the traditional male / female power relationship remains in place even though the woman is the harasser. The fact that she proposed the bargain does not challenge the structures of sexual politics and sexual economics, it merely sustains them.

Women in positions superior to males at the workplace or in higher education do harass down. The incidence is rare, but it does happen. The male sexual prerogative dimension does not apply in these cases, which may be, in an ironic way, a sign of hope. If women, who have not had direct access to economic power in the same way men have had, have the personal capacity to misuse their power when they get it in the same way men do, that surely indicates the problem is structural not biological. Sexual harassment need not be a permanent part of the workplace if we can make it less beneficial to those who do it, whether male or female.

THE EXTENT OF THE PROBLEM

Sexual harassment is a pervasive problem. At least 50 percent of all working women have experienced one or more forms of sexual harassment. Where women are few in a male-dominated occupation, that percentage goes up to 75 percent.[31] The Women's Legal Defense Fund put the incidence of sexual harassment at about 70 percent.[32] The problem is magnified when the ordinary channels for complaint are closed because the perpetrator is one's supervisor. Barbara Gutek and Bruce Morasch published the results of a study conducted in Los Angeles County in which 45 percent of the women who had experienced one of the more blatant forms of sexual harassment said the initiator was a supervisor.[33] Under these conditions, the possibility of appealing to someone within the organization for support and justification is very difficult, sometimes impossible.

I believe Laura Evans has the proper perspective on the extent of the problem of sexual harassment: if the average working woman experiences sexual harassment at some point in her working life, then the perpetrator must be the average working male.[34] This means that sexual harassment is not an aberration, but a commonplace event. Mary Rowe refers to harassing behavior as only rarely litigable, yet it constitutes what she calls microinequities, the daily minutiae of sexism whose cumulative effect is to erect serious barriers to women's educational and economic advancement.[35] Congressman James N. Hanley of New York, who chaired the Subcommittee on Investigations of the House Committee on Post Office and Civil Service, and whose initiative led to a landmark study by the U. S. Merit Systems Protection Board in 1981, said, "Our preliminary investigation has shown that the problem [of sexual harassment] is not only epidemic, it is pandemic, an everyday, everywhere occurrence."[36] Clearly, sexual harassment is a significant and formidable barrier to employment equity for women.

THE EFFECTS OF SEXUAL HARASSMENT

Sexual harassment maintains the clumping of women in certain occupations, or in limited roles within occupations (horizontal and vertical segregation, respectively). This is the structural effect. How does sexual harassment function this way? It discourages women from taking initiative, from offering leadership, and from entering and staying in male-dominated occupations.

Women who have been harassed report that once sexual harassment begins their jobs are in serious jeopardy, whether or not they complain. In some cases the harasser is angered because the woman refuses his advances, in others she is fired for being a troublemaker after she complains. An employer who is complicit in harassment will begin to find fault with an employee's work in an attempt to justify firing her, and even when not officially fired, women are often pressured into leaving their jobs by supervisors or coworkers who make working conditions intolerable.

A woman who is fired or pressured to leave her job has special difficulty getting back on her feet economically. She will probably receive poor work evaluations and references, which damages her chances for new and better jobs. Furthermore, she loses the advantage of experience she might have over other candidates for promotion or training, and she also forfeits the sick pay and pension rights linked to years of service. Her self-image and self-confidence are damaged, making the prospects of a job hunt seem overwhelming.

Job loss is a serious economic effect of sexual harassment, but even women who do not lose their jobs suffer. Sexual harassment diminishes people's ability to work efficiently and destroys their ambition. When one has to spend time and energy steering clear of offending parties, this leaves less energy for concentration on tasks required by the job and drains enthusiasm for work. Those who fear losing their jobs because they will not accept sexual advances from a supervisor or coworker suffer emotional and physical stress. Women in these situations feel powerless or trapped, they become self-conscious about their appearance, they lose ambition and experience less job satisfaction, and their job performance is impaired. Feelings of intimidation, frustration, guilt, embarrassment, degradation, anger, and fear are all common reactions.[37] Results of such stress are sleeplessness, nervous stomach, migraines, depression, and loss of appetite or weight gain. In addition, women who are harassed are denied the opportunity to work and advance routinely on the strength of their job skills. They are passed up for raises and promotions for reasons that are not job-related.

From the employer's point of view, people who have been subjected to harassment may appear to be uninterested in a career and seem unreliable, with poor job performance, absenteeism, unexplained requests for transfer, and unwillingness to work outside normal hours. These consequences were said to have cost the U.S. federal government $189 million from May 1978 to May 1980.[38]

I have yet to see any attempt to calculate how much it costs those who face harassment.

No one has ever completely explained the higher rate of unemployment and job turnover among women.[39] Lin Farley, in one of the earliest published treatments of sexual harassment, hypothesized that the missing piece of the puzzle is sexual harassment.[40] I believe this hypothesis will someday be confirmed. To some degree, sexual harassment contributes to a cycle of downward mobility, unemployment, and poverty among women.

Sexual Harassment, Rights, and Justice

The first response to sexual harassment must be, of course, clear recognition that it is wrong. It is wrong because perpetrators prevent people in the workplace from having their due (whether an atmosphere conducive to work, their jobs, promotions, or credit for their work) on the basis of criteria that are irrelevant to their work—their gender or their willingness to defer or to provide sexual access. It is an offense against justice according to work. It is also wrong because of the psychological and economic consequences to workers subjected to unaccountable power plays, and because it threatens workers' capacities to satisfy their basic needs and those of their dependents.

The fact that workers should be protected against quid pro quo harassment is not controversial. No one has made a serious case that employers or supervisors should have the right to make hiring or promotion decisions on the basis of whether or not they are able to extort sexual favors.

However, resistance to public policy proscribing sexual harassment does exist. Early in the debate on the issue, writer Walter Berns was one of those who objected to the EEOC's defining sexual harassment as a form of sex discrimination, charging women and their dress with equal complicity for male misuse of power in instances of sexual harassment.[41] I think such objections to EEOC jurisdiction in economic and relational matters are compromised seriously by their reliance on the myth that when men are sexually aroused they are not (and should not be) responsible for their behavior. That myth is one among many ways of blaming women for male misuse of power.

There is room for ambiguity in the hostile environment form of harassment, in that what some might see as normal male behavior might be interpreted as threatening by female coworkers. With regard to hostile environment harassment, therefore, there is currently some debate about whether the reigning rubric under which it falls should be civil rights or civil liberties.

In general terms, sexual harassment is treated by the courts as an offense against women's civil rights, as the law prohibiting it is the 1964 Civil Rights Act. There is an ongoing and deeply rooted tension between the legal treatment of atmospheric sexual harassment and the right to freedom of speech of the harassers, which is protected by the First Amendment to the U.S. Constitution. The tension is between a civil rights approach, rooted in antidiscrimination law and concerned with injuries of stigma and humiliation, and a civil liberties approach, rooted in a concern to protect freedom of speech against censorship, which limits the interference of government. This tension can be understood as a difference in priority between preserving individual rights and establishing and extending equality.

Some advocates of the civil liberties approach favor a very limited interpretation of hostile environment harassment in order to limit government intrusion into citizens' expressions of speech, particularly political expression. It is a protected right to hold a political opinion against gender equality, this view holds, even when such opinions are expressed in the workplace: the targets of sexist or racist speech should use their own rights to freedom of speech to combat discrimination, and the marketplace of ideas should be the arena in which harassing speech is controlled.[42]

Even those whose first priority is to protect freedom of speech acknowledge, however, that there are limits to the exercise of this right. Nadine Stroessen, arguing the position of the American Civil Liberties Union, specifies three situations that call for such limits: if harassing speech is an essential element of violent or unlawful conduct, if it is likely to cause an immediate injury by its very utterance, or if it is addressed to a captive audience unable to avoid assaultive messages.[43]

The question of what constitutes violent conduct, immediate injury, or a captive audience is the stuff of court cases, where the standard of the "reasonable man" is often relied upon. I believe that if the courts could see that the universe for women includes unprecedented levels of violence against girls and women, including rape and pornography, the courts would consistently view ambiguous incidents to constitute a hostile environment in the workplace from the point of view of a *reasonable woman*, as there is now precedent to do. Women must constantly judge whether harassing conduct is a prelude to violent sexual assault or employment discrimination.[44] Men do not experience these forms of speech or behavior as limiting their efforts in the workplace to the extent women do. The effect on women of harassing speech and behavior is violent to our sense of personhood, causes immediate or eventual economic dislocation, and finds us a captive audience when at work.

Ultimately, the resolution of the tension between the protection of civil liberties and the protection of civil rights must be a moral judgment, debated publicly and referenced to this particular historical situation. On the face of it, both freedom of speech and civil rights must remain protected; we need to find a compromise for our historical period. I would argue that the existing consequences for women and children of sexual harassment, including hostile environment harassment, are systemic in nature, linked to women's subordination in the patriarchal home and the patriarchal workplace. For now, the protection of women's civil rights should have priority, for the sake of women, our children, and the common good, because sexual harassment is a barrier to economic justice that functions in the whole society. Rights to freedom of speech are not thereby nullified. We must continue to protect them, but when they come into conflict with women's civil rights, the limit on men's freedom to express harassing views to women does not result in their suffering harm comparable to the effects on women of such harassment. In another time, with a different historical configuration, if women no longer experience more sexual violence than men and have an equal share of the benefits and liabilities of the economic order, that decision can be revisited.

Responses and Responsibilities

Social policy to address sexual harassment is already in place; it is Title VII of the Civil Rights Act of 1964, the same act which provides the basis for affirmative action, which is also a piece of addressing this problem, as later discussion will show. We may need better support for and implementation of this act, but the legal structure is in place to confront the problem. The work that remains ahead of us will take the form of changes in our attitudes about the sex roles undergirding sexual harassment, as well as workplace policies that bring us into clearer conformity with the law.

To stop sexual harassment, both women and men have some work to do. Men bear a particular responsibility to educate themselves about harassment, not only because they benefit most from women's intimidation in the workplace, and not only because they are most often the perpetrators of harassment, but also, according to researcher Heather Hemming, because they may need to sort out the differences between anger, warmth, and eroticism. Hemming maintains that men tend to confuse both aggression and warmth with eroticism, while women are more likely to distinguish among the three emotions; if a woman expresses anger to a man whose attention is unwanted, he may interpret that anger as erotic and his own anger as sexual attraction.[45]

Unfortunately, women will usually be point persons for change, however, because it is women who have to decide whether to name a given situation as harassment and convince their superiors and coworkers that it is.[46] For those who have taken the first and necessary step of identifying their experience as sexual harassment, what is required is stepping out of the "feminine" role of passivity, avoidance, and nurturance. Conflict and confrontation may be the only way to stop the unwanted behavior, and "nice girls" haven't been coached in either.

Economist Mary P. Rowe, who has written on sexual harassment for the *Harvard Business Review*, recommends a three-part letter to the harasser in which the writer states the facts as she or he sees them, describes the feelings evoked by the offense and the damage done, and specifies what the writer would like to have happen next. In Rowe's experience, in nearly all cases where such a letter is delivered the harassment stops, and if it does not, the letter is valuable for a complaint procedure or as legal evidence.[47] The virtue of this procedure is that it does not require a face-to-face showdown, yet it leaves a record of the troubling behavior and the author's desire that the behavior stop. Whether by the written word or in person, it must be communicated directly to the harasser that the problematic behavior is inappropriate and unwanted, and this step may take a great deal of courage.

If the initial communication is not successful, it may be most appropriate to escalate the confrontation to threats of exposure and/or to form alliances with others who might have been harassed by the same person. A group confrontation of the harasser may help.

If these informal techniques are not effective or appropriate, it will be necessary to take the case to the formal level, involving upper administration, initiating complaint procedures, filing a complaint with the union or with the state's equal employment opportunity agency.[48] There are some cases where it is most effective to take a friend for support and go directly to the top for administrative intervention in a bad situation. Confronting harassment requires tactics that will prevent retaliation, if possible.

Women also need to educate themselves about harassment, in particular with regard to feelings of guilt if we are harassed. Guilt is an appropriate response to having done something wrong, but it is not appropriate when you haven't and someone else has; yet many people when harassed feel automatically guilty, that somehow they must have brought it on themselves.

It is important that women educate themselves about the wider implications of harassment because when women blame themselves for harassing incidents they are less likely to report those incidents to someone in authority or to peers ("I thought it would be held against me") often out of concern about protecting the harasser ("I didn't want to hurt the person who bothered me").[49] This can allow the harasser to victimize other women.

This fact reminds us that confronting traditional sex roles is a very important piece of envisioning and creating a just economy for women. Sociologists Inger Jensen and Barbara Gutek found that women who hold to traditional sex roles are more likely than women who do not to hold women responsible for incidents of sexual harassment, to blame themselves if they have been subjected to harassment, and to fail to report the incident to someone in authority, coworkers, or friends. Therefore, educational programs about sexual harassment per se may not be effective in stopping such behavior. Such programs are helpful in providing ground rules for appropriate communicative styles, and, when mandated by upper management, for helping to provide a culture for a given organization that welcomes competence in women; however, more fundamental discussion about changing sex roles in our society is also required.[50] If "woman" means submissive, passive, nonaggressive, and fearful, and "man" means dominant, aggressive, adventurous, opportunistic, and proud of sexual ability, then sexual harassment can only be natural.

One of the best ways to guarantee that men and women have a relatively equal sensitivity to what constitutes sexual harassment is to integrate all work groups. Gender integration on the job is a consistent predictor that sexual harassment will be infrequent.[51] When women and men have equal power on the job, friendly and equitable relationships are more likely to result. Blatant experiences of sexual pressure will diminish and ambiguous incidents can be controlled since retaliation can occur in a joking context. This is why affirmative action programs are necessary for the diminishing of sexual coercion on the job. "Tokens" are always vulnerable, and the need for affirmative action will remain as long as there is evidence of sexual segregation of occupations. This means unions and managers have a mandate to integrate work units whenever a job category is clearly marked by gender segregation. It will be a mark of movement toward economic justice when there are no longer "men's jobs" and "women's jobs," only jobs to be done.

chapter four

Domestic Violence

O BE SEVERELY hurt, physically or psychologically, by the same people who nurture and love us runs counter to every expectation of the word "home." And yet domestic violence does happen to men and women, as children and as adults. In this chapter I will focus on the battering of adults, particularly of adult women.

Domestic violence is coercive and frightening behavior in the home or in intimate relationships, or among people who have been intimately related. This behavior may involve *physical abuse*, including assaults with weapons, assault with the batterer's own body, sleep interference or deprivation of heat or food; *sexual abuse*, including rape, sex on demand, or sexual withholding; *property abuse*, such as arson, pet abuse, stealing or destruction of property; *threats* to commit any of these abuses; *economic control*, including control over income and the assets of the partner, interfering with employment or education; *emotional abuse*, involving humiliation, degradation, lying, isolation, withholding of critical information, withholding of approval, appreciation, or affection as punishment, and continual criticism.[1]

That emotional abuse is a form of domestic violence may come as a revelation to many women and men alike. Although we tend to define domestic violence in terms of acts of bodily injury or harmful physical contact against a person or property, such acts do not constitute a series of isolated blow-ups, but they are a part of a process of deliberate intimidation intended to coerce the victim to do the will of the perpetrator. This process may not involve physical contact with the victim, since wall-punching, table-pounding, and verbal threats can achieve the same results as blows to the head. Domestic violence includes any acts that cause its victims to do something they do not want to do, prevent them from doing something they want to do, or cause them to be afraid for their safety or even for their lives.[2]

The Extent of the Problem

Surgeon General Antonia C. Novello called domestic violence an extensive, pervading, and entrenched problem in the United States.[3] It is the second leading cause of injuries to all women, and the leading cause of injuries to women ages fifteen to forty-four. More than 4 million women a year in the United States are severely assaulted by their husbands, boyfriends, or ex-partners. At least 25 percent of women will be attacked by their partners at some point in their lives, and three studies put that figure at 60 to 70 percent.[4] Between 10 and 20 percent of women suffer severe, chronic abuse.[5] One in three women who enter an emergency room has been abused, and 23 percent of pregnant women seeking prenatal care have experienced domestic violence. In 1990, more than 800 women were killed by their husbands, and 400 more were killed by their boyfriends.[6]

Domestic violence against women has become so prevalent that the American Medical Association has determined that physicians should routinely question female patients about whether they have been abused. The AMA's senior vice president for medical education and science, M. Roy Schwarz, said in 1992 that domestic violence had been a medical concern for decades, and that in the previous twenty years the problem had gotten worse rather than better.[7] As corrobation of the severity of this trend, the Council on Scientific Affairs of the AMA noted that while the percent of men murdered by unmarried romantic partners had fluctuated, the rate at which women were killed by their partners had increased sharply from 1976 through 1987.[8]

Domestic violence toward adults is, then, primarily a problem of assaults on women. Although some surveys suggest women are as likely to perpetrate at least one act of aggression as men, those surveys do not measure acts that are undertaken in self-defense. Not only do men perpetrate more aggressive and severe actions against their female partners than women do against male partners, they are more likely to perpetrate multiple aggressive actions during a single incident. On average, men have greater physical strength than their female partners, making the outcomes of male violence likely to be more severe than the outcomes of female violence; women are much more likely to be injured by their male partners than men are by their female partners.[9] In 95 percent of spouse abuse cases, the abuse is inflicted by the male partner on the female partner.[10] So while both men and women can be victims or perpetrators of abuse, overwhelmingly women suffer more effects of violence than men do. We must not shirk from focusing on the social problem of domestic violence against women.

Domestic violence cuts across all racial, religious, educational, and socioeconomic lines. Victims share no psychological or cultural characteristics. However, a woman's class and status influences her access to medical care. "Women of higher socioeconomic status are more likely to seek care in private practice settings, while low-income women are more likely to go to clinics and emergency departments."[11] Class and status make a difference in how women cope with abuse, but do not determine whether they will escape it.

While the focus of this discussion is on heterosexuals, gay people do not escape the dynamics of violence in their intimate relationships. Women too beat each other in the context of intimate relationships, although we do not know the rate of such violence.[12] Lesbian battering takes the same forms as male battering, but may also include homophobic control, such as threatening to tell the family, friends, employer, police, or religious organization that the partner is lesbian. Gay male abuse takes the same forms.

Lesbian or gay male battering is no more mutual than heterosexual battering. Body size and strength may be more equal in female-female and male-male violence, but in the reported cases one partner is clearly the perpetrator. The motivation for a lesbian batterer is the same as for men who batter—to feel powerful and establish control over another person. Victims of such battering are as reluctant to admit or expose the problem as heterosexual victims are, and lesbian abusers are as resistant to rehabilitation as male abusers, whether heterosexual or gay.

The basis of lesbian and gay battering is the same as that for all other abuse: the acceptance of violence as a form of power and control. Significantly, some theorists argue that internalized homophobia, the additional factor in lesbian and gay battering, is built upon the belief structure of misogyny, the hatred and devaluation of women.[13]

The Effects of Domestic Violence

The experience of domestic violence is psychologically devastating. From a man who has courted her and seemed protective, solicitous and admiring, a woman receives what may be her first experience of being hit, slapped, kicked, or beaten. To make sense out of the experience, many women have one or more of the same thoughts: he is not the sort of person who would beat a woman, and I am not the sort of person who would be beaten—it was a mistake, and it won't happen again; I must have done something to upset him when he was particularly needy, but if I continue to love him and prove to him the strength of my commitment, he won't make that mistake again; I can help him reform.

Some women have very few thoughts at all after the first time they've been abused physically by their intimate partner. They are in shock, numb. Since the experience was unbelievable, they suffer disorientation and lose trust in their ability to understand the world. Most at stake is their self-respect.

Many battered women express a genuine love for their partners and a commitment to try to make their relationships work. Because love and self-esteem for women have been associated with self-denial and the capacity for sacrifice, there can be very long periods in their lives when women live with violence. Indeed, it may take a long time for both partners to acknowledge that their relationship is violent.

A political model for understanding how abuse works is the torture of political prisoners. A man who batters a woman uses the same methods that torturers do. The woman, like the political prisoner, is isolated from all social support; her perception is monopolized by the batterer; he induces exhaustion and debility; he threatens her, her children, her pets, or her property; he occasionally indulges her, but then demonstrates his omnipotence by beating her, following her, or calling her crazy; he degrades her; he enforces trivial demands to develop in her a habit of compliance.[14] The physical violence itself can be identical to torture: sleep deprivation, burns, electric shock, bondage, semistarvation, choking, near-drowning, exposure, mutilation, rape, and forcible rape with objects or animals.[15]

Political theory about the phenomenology of terrorism is also a useful resource for the study of family violence. Terrorism disorients people because terrorist acts are arbitrary and unpredictable. There appears to be no pattern, cause, or understandable link between what a person does and what happens to him or her.[16] In such situations, human beings become cautious and conformist. This strategy may succeed in delaying violence, but it will not stop it.

The medical model of trauma can help us understand the effects of domestic violence on the victim. Women abused by male partners experience fear, anxiety, fatigue, sleeping and eating disturbances, intense startle reactions, and physical complaints long after the abuse has occurred. They may become dependent and suggestible and find it difficult to make decisions. Because women abused by male partners often have legal, financial, and parenting relationships with their assailants, their decisions to protect themselves have consequences for the other most important relationships in their lives. The effects of the trauma are exacerbated by the fact that the aggressor is someone they may love and depend on.[17]

Psychologist Lenore Walker describes the cyclical nature of battering behavior, with a tension-building phase, an explosion or acute battering incident, and a calm, loving respite.[18] Couples that experience one of these cycles are likely to experience another, then another, with the time between each cycle becoming shorter and shorter. When men use physical abuse against women to coerce their loyalty, they know at some level that the loyalty they receive is compromised by fear, but they are willing to live with that. An abusive man may forbid his partner from seeing or talking on the phone with friends, old or new, or family. He may insist that she quit her job. He may deprive her of a checkbook or money, and keep her from all knowledge of their financial affairs. He may lock her in the house when he leaves her and take the car keys. In sum, many abusive men try to possess their partners in every possible way.

Fear of retaliation keeps many women from walking out. This fear is often well founded. If a battered woman does leave, the batterer may go to her family and friends and abuse them if he suspects they are hiding her. He may go to schools or baby sitters to find her children and hold them hostage until she gives in and says she will return. If she works, he may go to her job and hunt her down to beat her—or kill her—when she leaves. Terrorism is not too horrible a description of the lethal possessiveness expressed by violent men.

People who are not in abusive relationships often blame the battered woman for her batterer's behavior, since "she should have left him"; this misplaced blame thrives on ignorance about the numbers of women who do leave and the consequences they face at the hands of their batterers. Karen Steinhauser, chief deputy district attorney in the Denver District Attorney's Office, investigates and prosecutes crimes involving incest, sexual abuse of children, and domestic violence. She describes the danger a woman faces when she decides to leave a battering man who may kill her if she *doesn't* leave.

> The most dangerous time for victims is after they have left a battering relationship. We have had more homicides at that time, after they have left. So, women think in terms of survival, not safety. And their way of thinking is, "If I stay in this situation, I might get beat or hit, but that is a lot better than being out somewhere and not knowing if he is going to be around the corner waiting for me." It's the not

knowing what will happen from day to day. That's how victims think. They think in terms of what they need to do to survive.[19]

Why Men Abuse

A man beats a woman to maintain control in the relationship, to remind her that the relationship will proceed in the way he wants or he will resort to physical force.[20] The fact that wife assault is unlikely to be severely punished allows the behavior to continue.

The control a batterer wants is not primarily for purposes of labor exploitation. If it were, batterers would not hurt women to the extent that they have to be hospitalized or cannot get out of bed for days. Rather, control gives the batterer prestige, self-esteem, and self-worth. Battering is a way of making the point that women belong to men: he believes he has the right to beat her.

Many batterers explain their intensely damaging behavior by saying that they were out of control. Yet many men are violent only with their partners, in the privacy of their homes. Sometimes they select carefully which area of a woman's body to abuse; they usually do not kill, and can exercise substantial control when threatened with jail sentences. They may act "out of control," but most batterers know what they are doing.[21]

The man who batters is typically described as having a dual personality, very charming at times and cruel at others.[22] His charm and verbal skills are well developed for his social life and his job. But batterers as a group tend to be less verbally assertive with their wives or partners than nonabusive men and lack the verbal skills to express their personal needs. In fact, their personal style is often to be the "strong, silent type" in their families, where, of all places, they should have the psychological space to express themselves through verbal and body language rather than force. Abusive men are usually very emotionally dependent on their partners and are quite jealous and possessive of them.[23] Many women report that when they have tried to leave abusive partners their abusers have said, "I'd kill you before I'd let you leave me." About 1,200 men a year carry through on their threats.[24]

Factors that contribute to the abuse of women by men include work-related stress, financial problems, unemployment of males, jealousy, alcohol and drug use, pregnancy, male underachievement and a job of lower socioeconomic status than the partner's, marital conflict, and an intergenerational cycle of violence.[25] However, none of these factors have ever been shown to *cause* a man to beat the woman in his love life.[26] Men who have work-related stress sometimes play basketball after work. Marital conflicts are not always dealt with by physical force. Some men who as boys witnessed family violence vow they will never do that, and don't.

The question to be posed is, Why did that man think it was all right for him to relieve his stress in this particular way? Asking this question may help us to understand that there is no excuse for domestic violence. Abusive men need more than anything to be accountable for their behavior to a culture and a neighborhood that will say—and mean—there is no justification for even "a little" violence. No matter what she may have said or done, no woman deserves to be beaten. It is only a male-supremacist culture that believes a marriage license is a license to abuse.

SOCIETAL ENABLERS OF DOMESTIC VIOLENCE

The power structure of a marriage or partnership is related directly to the social and economic status as well as the relative physical sizes of its two members. Since men generally hold higher-paying jobs with more occupational prestige, have a traditional role of dominance within society, and are typically stronger than women, they have a greater tendency toward assuming a position of power within marriage.[27] In order for men to dominate, women must be dominated. Women's subordinate status has long been associated with domestic violence, because physical force is ultimate recourse to keep subordinate groups in their place.[28]

Violence against women exists in various forms in everyday life in *all* societies, and there is a growing international consensus that it can no longer be dismissed as something private and beyond the scope of government responsibility.[29] Yet changes in law and its application are insufficient by themselves without cultural reform specific to the peoples involved, though advocates for women can support each other across international boundaries.

In the United States and other Western countries, appeals for economic justice for women are taken as lightly as they are in part because we have a social memory that a man's wife is his property; we cannot take seriously the question of increasing women's access to property because women *are* property in our barely articulated historical memory.

Our country's laws and institutions were shaped by the cultures of Western Europe, which in turn drew on principles from biblical times. Thus we must examine attitudes toward women in these periods before we can understand the violence against them in our own day. That violence is not new. For example, in 1878, Francis Power Cobbe wrote in *Wife Torture in England*, "The notion that a man's wife is his property in the sense in which a horse is his property . . . is the total root of incalculable evil and misery."[30]

Under English common law, a husband had the legal right to use force against his wife in order to ensure that she fulfilled her wifely obligations: the consummation of the marriage, cohabitation, maintenance of conjugal rights, sexual fidelity, and general obedience and respect for his wishes.[31] Through the seventeenth, eighteenth, and nineteenth centuries, social norms allowed a man to use force against his wife as long as he did not exceed certain limits. (The origin of the expression "rule of thumb" is that the stick used to administer punishment to a wife was not to exceed the thickness of a man's thumb.)

The nineteenth-century English customs Cobbe described were in part the legacy of the gender power relations reflected in the Hebrew Scriptures and the New Testament. Rarely written from a woman's point of view, these scriptures reveal a world in which a man had meaning and significance as the embodiment of his family, its head, and its representative in dealing with outsiders. As the patriarch, his task was to maintain the family's wealth and community standing, and the task of all other members of the family was to serve the interests of the patriarch. Wives, children, and slaves were all property of the male heads of household, and of his family.[32]

This conception of women as property remained stable over a

very long period of time, through the New Testament era and further. According to New Testament scholar L. William Countryman, there were some changes in detail. In the centuries before and after Jesus, women were occasionally accepted as something like religious equals, but wives continued to be a particular class of property, whose function was to produce heirs and administer the husband's household.[33]

As part of the biblical heritage of Christianity, some aspects of this worldview were incorporated into the law in Western Europe in later eras. Historian Lawrence Stone describes the legal situation of women in the restricted patriarchal nuclear family which prevailed in England from 1550 to 1700:

> By marriage, the husband and wife became one person in law—and that person was the husband. He acquired absolute control of all his wife's personal property, which he could sell at will. . . . This legal subjection of women to husbands or fathers was the reason why the franchise was always restricted to male householders. . . . Women were self-evidently not free persons, and therefore were no more eligible for the vote than children.[34]

Stone finds that the patriarchal family was encouraged in those societies with strong authoritarian state systems, as authoritarian monarchy and domestic patriarchy form a congruent and mutually supportive complex of ideas and social systems. He also views the patriarchal family as not primarily a religious phenomenon dependent upon a particular type of Christianity but a regional cultural feature common to Catholic Christians, Orthodox Christians, and Moslems around the Mediterranean basin. Middle- and upper-class patriarchy in sixteenth- and early seventeenth-century England also had roots in a different religious tradition; that of the Reformation, which included the doctrine of the priesthood of all believers, one consequence of which was the view that the husband and father became the spiritual as well as the secular head of the household.[35]

In the United States this legacy was transmitted largely through European and English religious and legal traditions to people of European extraction as well as to native people and people of African descent. In Latin America, the Spanish Christian influence ensured a patriarchal family structure. Religious expressions of patriarchy are affected by geography, period, and culture. Transformation of these religious ideas may take specifically religious form, but such change will need buttressing by social and economic changes.

Like the patriarchal family, wife beating has a long history. Although the right to chastise physically has disappeared from the common law, the masculine and feminine sex roles that accompanied such behavior persist. Sex roles are at one and the same time *social* expectations that are applied to persons of a given biological sex, and, when internalized, *personal* experiences of ourselves as "masculine" or "feminine." Sex roles vary dramatically from society to society, but every society has them.[36] The gender system in any society consists of assignments of sex roles, which individuals accept, reject, and tailor in various ways.

In the United States, while a range of cultures interact, the desirable characteristics for a woman still often correspond to those of a good domestic servant: concerned about others (particularly men and children), willing to defer to men, nurturant, emotional rather than rational, ill at ease with leadership.

Masculine sex roles are characterized by expressions of power (not collaboration), dominance, and competition. In effect, the masculine role is to manage the servants, to be in control. For their part, men are not always aware of their need to control; rather, they are socialized to feel uncomfortable when not in control. Women play a role in maintaining this psychosocial dynamic when we feel uncomfortable with women's leadership. These sex roles can inhibit or prevent intimacy among men or between women and men, as being in control is incompatible with the vulnerability intimacy requires. Difficulty in establishing intimate relationships is one of the principal characteristics of men who abuse their wives.

The Economic Context

Domestic violence has broad economic as well as psychological effects. According to the Bureau of National Affairs, employers lose $3 billion to $5 billion annually because of absenteeism, employee turnover, and health care expenses resulting from domestic violence.[37] This estimate is probably low, because domestic beatings are rarely mentioned by employees as the reason for missing work, and the total economic costs of domestic violence should also include the wages lost by injured victims and the costs of social services for them. Until an effort is made to identify what domestic violence costs women, we will have to intuit the costs by looking at facets of women's situations and imagining what the aggregate might be.[38]

Not only does domestic violence have economic effects, economic dependence can allow domestic violence to continue. Women who are both unemployed and partners in long-term relationships are the least likely to leave abusive men. This is why long-term treatment alternatives for battered women should focus on both economic and psychological independence.

If the goal of a healthy relationship is interdependence, as Lenore Walker suggests—that is, both people being capable of either independent or dependent behavior within a relationship, as appropriate—then women need skills to enable them to be economically independent at any time. We must be capable of standing alone and meeting our needs economically as well as emotionally in order to truly choose to be in an interdependent relationship. In other words, the precondition of mutuality in a relationship is the possibility of being autonomous and independent.

Domestic violence works in several ways to make and keep women economically vulnerable. First, violent men often discourage their female partners from working, getting education, or seeking job training because they want their partners to be dependent economically on them, and in an abusive relationship, a woman loses the self-respect and self-confidence necessary to go into the job market, learn new skills, and meet challenges. Second, battered women in the paid labor force lose days at work, hiding or healing from injuries, and irregular work attendance can jeapordize a woman's standing in her position and compromise her wages. Third, if a woman leaves an abusive relationship before she has the social support system to help her establish stability in a new living environment, she may end up on the street with the crazy-making pressures of no home or social claim on the rest of the community. (There are estimates that between 40 and 50 percent of homeless women and children are on the street because of domestic violence.[39]) Fourth, even when an abused woman makes a new life for herself (and her children), she will often have to leave behind possessions she will have to replace in order to avoid being entangled with her abuser or endangering herself and her children.

Domestic violence is rooted in the expectation of women's servitude and functions to steer us in that direction, both psychologically and economically.

What Must Be Done: The Law and Public Policy

Domestic violence violates women's inherent dignity, freedom, and bodily integrity—our right to be free from bodily harm, a right that belongs to all U.S. citizens under the Constitution.[40]

Furthermore, in the context of international codes of basic human rights, the failure to prosecute domestic violence constitutes a human rights abuse.[41] That so many nations—our own included—have neglected or been slow to recognize equality before and equal protection of the law without regard to sex is the result of approaching supposedly gender-neutral international law from social structures that are pervaded with gender bias, particularly the bias that men act in the public sphere and should be protected by law, while women operate in the private sphere where intervention of the law is inappropriate.[42]

The first public policy arena that must be considered to stop domestic violence in this country is that of public safety and the criminal justice system. Women *should* be able to rely on the force of social pressure to deter male violence and to hold men accountable should it nevertheless occur; there should be a shared social assumption that all forms of domestic violence are unthinkable. Until that day, however, the next best form of deterrence is the threat of external control in the form of arrest and conviction.

Some states are exploring new ways to increase rates of arrest for batterers. One of these new approaches involves training health care providers to diagnose and help battered women, providing not just medical care but also a sympathetic ear, alternatives to returning home, and referrals for counseling, shelter, and legal services. Without training, health care providers can be ambivalent about becoming involved, for a variety of reasons, among them the possibility that they themselves may have been subjected to domestic violence and not be comfortable with the close identification with their patients.[43] But specific training and information addressed to nurses and physicians can help them to identify any sources of personal discomfort and neutralize them, and to play a positive role more lasting than patching a person up and returning her to a bad situation.

Some states have taken this a step further and concluded that health care providers should be required to make a report to law enforcement when domestic violence is suspected. As of 1994, seven states had such mandatory reporting laws.[44] These laws are controversial because of their implications for both health care providers and the assaulted women. Medical professionals argue that reporting a domestic violence incident to police without helping the woman in other ways is not sufficient, and that they lack the training and backup to aid or refer these patients to social services. The injured woman, on the other hand, has sought medical care, not police involvement, and "must-report" policies take from her the choice about whether to involve the police; the batterer may have threatened to harm her further if she tells anyone about the abuse, and she may be left with him after the police investigate, should there be insufficient evidence to arrest.

In short, mandatory reporting policies themselves create new stresses. They may be justifiable if they yield more accurate statistics about the number of domestic assaults that occur (which will help argue for more public support for social services and sensitize police departments to the actual needs of women in abusive relationships), however, mandatory reporting violates patient autonomy, confidentiality, and informed consent. Some advocates for assaulted women doubt that such policies are the best means to accomplish data collection and documentation about domestic assault, to improve health care providers' responses to abused patients, or even to aid law enforcement in criminal prosecution.[45] Therefore, careful attention to mandatory reporting policies is warranted, and such policies should be constructed carefully by health care providers, law enforcement officials, and women's advocacy groups together.

A further effort to eliminate the battering of women involves "must-arrest" policies. Recognizing that women are often financially dependent upon their batterers and that they are frequently coerced by them to drop charges should they involve the police, some police departments and district attorneys' offices are removing the onus from the abused woman, defining domestic abuse as a threat to public safety and proceding to arrest and take the perpetrator to court, even when the battered woman refuses to testify, if there is sufficient cause on the basis of evidence available to the officers called to the site of violence. The moral issues raised by these policies are different from those involved in the mandatory reporting policies discussed above because the threatened person has identified her situation as one requiring assistance from police, and because it is the nature of law enforcement to mete out consequences to those who engage in criminal activity. One of the reasons men continue to batter is that they think they can get away with it without suffering significant consequences; time in jail makes an impact on men who are law abiding in every other way, as many batterers are.[46]

As part of a trend toward "criminalizing" battering, must-arrest policies have proven to be a way to use social resources to protect women. Prior to 1985, when Denver implemented a must-arrest policy, Denver police made about 1,700 arrests a year for domestic violence; since 1985 they have increased arrests to over 5,000 per year.[47] Must-arrest policies have required a reorientation of priorities in police departments that adopt them, but without them, women's constitutional rights to equal protection are violated because they are treated differently than other classes of victims who have been assaulted.

It should be emphasized that must-arrest policies and vigorous, "do-not-drop" prosecution by district attorneys' offices are not efforts to make a new range of behaviors criminal—assault has always been criminal behavior. "Criminalization" refers to an increasing awareness among law enforcement and the judiciary that the laws against assault should be enforced equitably across gender lines.

Since domestic violence against women is not random, but is in part directed at women to prevent them from being social and economic equals with men, it is not enough to focus remedy solely on attaining equal protection of the law. This is another instance in which gender neutrality, when it is a value or ideal, must be aided by compensatory social change on behalf of women, supported by a redirection of social wealth.

In particular, public policy must support temporary safe houses or shelters for battered women and their children, and this is the second arena of public policy needed to stop domestic violence. Typically, a woman will return to an abusive relationship three, four, or five times before finally making a total break.[48] Shelters, second-stage or transitional housing, and the social support of people in these shelters make that break possible for many women. People associated with shelters and safe houses for battered women and their children report that when women are allowed to stay for at least three weeks to a month they are more likely to become independent. Women often need time with a variety of social service agencies and advocates to help them begin to use these services to get the income, housing, child care, job training, and medical help and therapy they need to achieve health and wholeness. A woman cannot file for financial assistance from safety net agencies unless she has filed for divorce and established her own domicile, but to establish that domicile takes money. It is heartbreaking to see women returning to their husbands because they do not see any possibilities for achieving economic independence for themselves and their children.

There are now more than 1,300 refuges or shelters for battered women in the 3,200 counties of the United States (the first such refuge was established in 1971, in England), yet every time a shelter opens it is filled quickly. Only one out of four battered women gets the assistance she needs from a safe house.[49] The support of refuges and second-stage refuges for longer-term residence gives women the opportunity to live with peers who are also learning economic and psychological independence, and will remain an important social policy objective for some time.

Thirdly, we must fund public education about domestic violence, research into its causes and solutions, and training for battered women's advocates.[50] Efforts to pass federal legislation for this purpose have been inadequate or unsuccessful, and slow in coming. However, the Violence Against Women Act, incorporated into the 1994 Crime Bill, contains provisions to encourage law enforcement to develop more effective policies regarding domestic violence, including education and training about mandatory arrest policies. In the arena of electoral politics, the idea of government intervention in marriage, even at the risk of permitting violence to continue, has been nearly taboo.[51] This protection of the (patriarchal) family at the expense of the well-being of women must be challenged in the arena of public debate. It would help such efforts for the churches to develop a biblical theology of family as Jesus' community of equals, to counter the patriarchal model.

Fourthly, we must encourage cultural restoration movements such as the one undertaken by the Rosebud Sioux. Confronting the high level of domestic violence on the Rosebud reservation, tribal leaders attibuted the phenomenon to the abandonment of their native culture in favor of the colonizers' European culture. To combat domestic violence, they have initiated a restoration movement to remember the Sioux ways before colonization—ways of respect for women, enculturated in matriarchal and matrilineal structures. No Sioux woman before colonization would have been expected to submit to a man who beat her. No Sioux man would have believed that he was entitled to use physical force against his partner. Before Europeanization, womanhood did not require acquiescence to male power, and manhood did not require enforcing it.[52]

Inheritors of other traditions must evaluate religion, family structure, economy, and other cultural factors within their communities by the criterion Do these institutions and belief systems support the dignity of women? Within the Christian religious perspective, we can claim a tradition that values the equality of women and men in the life and teachings of Jesus and the very earliest house churches. There are movements to celebrate the full personhood of women in nearly every major religious tradition today, even though the social and religious equality of women is not a dominant teaching of any of them.

*   *   *

Finally, all educational, welfare, and family policy efforts must be evaluated in terms of whether they support the changing aspects of family life that help to equalize the balance of power between husband and wife, men and women. These changes include the rise in the average age at first marriage, the increase in the average age for having a first child, the decline in the number of children per family, and the decrease in the number of unwanted children.[53] The entrance of women into the paid labor force has probably been the most significant cause of these family structure changes. Because full-time housewives experience a higher rate of domestic abuse than do women in the paid labor force, this particular aspect should not be underemphasized; policies that support equity in the labor force can help support women's equality in marriage or partnership and increase their possibility of being self-sufficient. Affirmative action is still required to increase the percentages of women obtaining bachelor's, graduate, and professional degrees or completing special training for the skilled trades; these measures will help address vertical segregation in the labor force. Comparable worth legislation is also necessary to address the horizontal segregation of the labor force.

Community-based child care, developed and staffed by adults whose work the community also values, is also an important component of women's economic independence. In addition to allowing battered women to get education, training, or work, child care can also offer resources for healthy nonviolent child rearing. Shelter workers report that one way peers help women prepare for independence is by teaching, through example and word, how to relate to children without abuse and stop the intergenerational cycle of violence. Child care centers have played a good role in providing education for parents, usually in the form of supportive suggestion but also by modeling.

Criminalization for violent offenders, a refuge for women and children in every county, more support for affirmative action legislation and comparable worth legislation to ensure equity for women in the paid labor force, and community-based child care—these are some of the public policies needed to put an end to domestic violence against women. The moral and political will for such policies could be nurtured and taught in religious communities. If they do not take initiative to confront the traditional bases for men using violence against their partners, or if they choose not to speak to the problem at all, then alternative arenas for women to worship will continue to grow. It is in these latter arenas that the memory is most vivid that women are powerful and beneficent, as God is.

Lesbian Identity

LESBIAN WOMEN ARE not exempt from the economic discrimination described in other chapters—they bear and raise children, face a greater risk of sexual harassment, and experience violence in intimate relationships—but they are also affected by discrimination against people who choose sexual relationships with people of the same sex. This chapter will explore the ways in which antigay policies affect lesbian women, as well as the ways in which lesbian women's economic situations may differ from those of heterosexual women, and will show why discrimination on the basis of sexual preference is unjust.

Who are lesbian women? A lesbian person is a woman who says she is a lesbian person. In the United States and most other industrialized nations, self-identified lesbians tend to be women who have clear and continuous patterns of relating—through attraction, fantasies, and behavior—to other women, and who have emotional and social preferences for a lifestyle with other women. However, this definition does not necessarily hold for other cultures, because lesban identity is expressed in different ways depending on the spheres of female activities and the networks characteristic of a given culture.

Women in all societies are expected to marry and bear children.[1] However, certain variables, such as the age of betrothal and marriage, rights to property, and the amount of power women have over such matters, will have a bearing on lesbian behavior. Anthropologist Evelyn Blackwood found that in societies where women have control over their productive activities and status, they will develop both formal and informal lesbian relations. (Formal relations are part of the social structure and take the form of bond friendship, sisterhoods, and woman-marriage; informal relations are those that do not extend beyond the immediate context, such as adolescent sex play and affairs among women in harems or polygynous households.) Where women lack power, they maintain only informal lesbian ties or build institutions outside the dominant culture.[2]

Women always have some control over their sexuality before, during, after, and in the absence of marriage, although the overall context across cultures and time remains one in which men control women's sexuality.[3] Even within strongly patriarchal societies, women are capable of forming alternative institutions that circumvent male control, particularly if women have an economic basis for such circumvention.[4] Blackwood believes the lesbian subculture that has developed in Western societies in the last eighty years is outside the social structure of the dominant culture and dependent upon the tolerance of that culture. However, recent instances of legal acknowledgement of domestic partnerships in certain areas of the United States, and the legalization of lesbian and gay marriages in Denmark (1989) and in Norway (1993), indicate a move toward more formal relationships in some Western countries.

The discussion of lesbian identity that follows is primarily relevant to the U.S. context and dependent upon studies of lesbian and gay experience that are largely, though not exclusively, concerned with the U.S. population.

It is impossible to pinpoint the number of lesbians in the United States. One commonly used estimate, attributed to Alfred Kinsey, is that about 10 percent of the population is homosexual and all societies are predominantly heterosexual. But Kinsey's own research, begun in the 1930s and continuing into the 1950s, indicated that 3 to 4 percent of men are exclusively homosexual, and about 2 percent of women are exclusively lesbian.[5] This figure can only be an estimate, because lesbian and gay identity is known only by asking people, who may or may not want to tell their truths. Furthermore, this figure does not include people who are bisexual, those who are predominantly heterosexual but have homosexual experiences, or those who are predominantly homosexual but have heterosexual experiences.

Kinsey's data, corroborated by Morton Hunt's data from the early 1970s, indicate that roughly 25 percent of American males and 15 percent of American females have had at least one homosexual experience, and a considerable number of other persons have responded erotically to persons of the same sex, but without physical contact.[6] For good reason, then, Alan Bell and Martin Weinberg, of the Institute for Sex Research (founded by Alfred Kinsey), have concluded that people are not necessarily either homosexual or heterosexual alone. Rather, each person responds to men and women in different ways and to different degrees.[7]

Significant numbers of lesbians have heterosexual experiences quite similar to those of heterosexual women, including dating and marrying men, but at some time in their lives they choose to relate to women rather than men. In the majority of cases, their first lesbian experience is initiated mutually with a partner in the same age group. Their relationships are not sexually promiscuous; lesbians enter, stay, and leave relationships in a process similar to that of any heterosexual couple. Nor are the great majority of lesbian relationships characterized by butch / femme roles. In spite of the prevailing stigma attached to lesbian relationships, lesbians manage their love relationships, friendships, jobs, and social lives in a variety of ways, and are comparable in their psychological adjustment to heterosexual women.[8]

Discrimination against Gays and Lesbians

Discrimination against lesbians and gay men includes employment discrimination, police harassment, prejudice in court cases involving child custody, housing discrimination, rejection by family members, limitations on freedom of association and speech, unequal protection under the law, physical violence, and homophobic rhetoric at all levels of the society.[9]

All of these forms of prejudice and discrimination may have economic implications. In most municipalities of the United

States, the civil rights of lesbians and gay men are not protected, and employers who dismiss, refuse to hire, or fail to promote lesbian women and gay men because of their sexual orientation are free from legal challenge or penalty.[10] When gay adult consensual sex is not protected with privacy rights, police harassment can send gay men to prison, thus preventing them from participating in the economy. In order to seek restitution or retribution in the courts from people who assault them, gay or lesbian people have to be willing to let their names be made public. Without civil rights protection against discrimination in housing, they may lose their apartments because of a landlord's homophobia.

In the United States, marriages between gay men and between lesbian women do not have legal standing. Marriage is regulated by state law, and every state's law explicitly or implicitly reserves marriage for people of the opposite sex.[11] If other kinds of domestic partnerships are not recognized in the law, corporations have little incentive to extend benefits to unmarried employees' domestic partners, although some have taken this step anyway.[12] Benefits available to a married employee and his or her spouse may include health and dental insurance for both partners, moving expenses for the household, library and gym privileges for both, parenting leave for the parent who did not give birth, leave to attend a funeral in the spouse's family, leave to attend to a sick member of the family, subsidized day care, discount travel for both, and more. When one employee is eligible for fewer benefits than another because she or he is not permitted to marry, and if the difference is not made up in wages, that employee is being paid less for doing the same work as performed by a married employee.[13] In this way states' laws precluding same-sex marriages favor the distribution of benefits to heterosexual married couples. Extension of employee benefits to all domestic partners is one way to redress the unfairness that results from limiting marriage to heterosexual partners. Such benefits are particularly important to lesbians, as women are traditionally in lower-paying positions with fewer employment benefits, and the likelihood that both partners would have benefits is lower than for gay male couples.[14]

Tax structures often reflect societal priorities, and both federal and state tax codes show no support for lesbian and gay committed relationships. Favorable tax treatment for transfer of property from one spouse to another is not available to lesbian or gay couples no matter how long they have have been together or how interdependent in their finances they are. A nonbiological coparent may be financially supporting a child, but cannot take advantage of a head-of-household deduction because she is not legally recognized as the child's parent.[15]

In addition, some life insurance companies refuse to allow policyholders to designate an unmarried partner as beneficiary. Many insurance companies deny coverage, set higher rates, or cancel policies because the policyholders are unmarried or because of their sexual orientation. Another discriminatory policy regards the laws giving crime victims and their economically dependent partners recourse against wrongdoers. If one's spouse is seriously injured or killed, one can sue for damages to the marriage, emotional trauma, or wrongful death. However, if a member of an unmarried couple is killed or maimed, the survivor, even if economically dependent upon the partner, has no recourse to sue.[16]

While some of the injustices stated above also apply to heterosexual unmarried partners, the violence directed against lesbian women and gay men is unlike anything that heterosexual unmarried partners experience. In all areas of their lives, lesbians and gays encounter violence directed at them because of their sexual orientation.[17]

This violence takes many forms, including physical beatings and slashings, destruction of cars and other property, robbery, social isolation (particularly perpetrated by parents of adolescent gay and lesbian persons), and hostile remarks and taunting. It is perpetrated by family members, former spouses, other relatives, and anonymous attackers, particularly adolescent males in groups. Even those who are not open about their sexual orientation may experience violence; for example, 21 percent of lesbian women and gay men who are not open to anyone in their workplace are attacked or abused. Fully 50 percent of lesbians and gays have been victims of antigay violence.[18]

The violation of gay men's and lesbians' bodies, their life plans, and their freedom of movement is paralleled in heterosexual experience only with respect to extreme forms of racism and domestic violence. Both gay bashing and domestic violence are systems of violence which if not condoned are certainly tolerated in our society.

The Economic Standing of Lesbians

Although they experience discrimination in a way that heterosexual women do not, lesbians as a group are in some respects better prepared to support themselves financially than heterosexual women are.[19] To begin with, lesbian women may be as much as nine times more likely than the general adult female population to have advanced education or professional degrees.[20]

Hilda Hidalgo's research on Puerto Rican lesbians in the United States provides an example that confirms this general picture. She found that 98 percent of Puerto Rican lesbians in the United States had completed high school, as opposed to only 33 percent of all Puerto Ricans in the country (ages fifteen to twenty-four). And while about 2 percent of Puerto Rican youth attend college, 12 percent of Hidalgo's lesbian respondents had done so, and 3 percent had graduate or professional degrees.[21] (About 14 percent of U.S. women have college diplomas, as was discussed in Chapter 2, so while Puerto Rican lesbians are more educated than other Puerto Rican women, their rate of college education is no higher than that of the general population of women in the United States.) Hidalgo also found that the median income of the Puerto Rican lesbian sample exceeded that of the general Puerto Rican population by 40 percent at least, and that the higher income could be attributed to lesbians' higher educational achievement.[22]

Lesbians come from every socioeconomic strata, but to the degree that women suspect early in life that they will not look to a well-educated male to support them, vocation in the paid labor force becomes more important to their life plans.

Work tends to be central, therefore, in the lives of lesbians to a larger degree than it is for heterosexual women. A number of studies show consistently that lesbians have stable work histories, are higher achievers than comparable heterosexual women, and have a serious commitment to work.[23] In work, lesbians have access to a means of economic survival and, in addition, a source of personal integrity, achievement, and strength. Although lesbians, like other women, seek emotional ties with coworkers more than men tend to do, lesbians are less likely than heterosexual women to have family obligations that pull them away from work commitments.[24] Although some lesbians are mothers and have many family responsibilities—and in the future this trend will likely increase—more lesbians do not have children than do at this time. In this respect, lesbians are more likely to have the kind of commitment to the workplace that has been associated with men.

Nevertheless, the sexist constraints of the workplace affect lesbians as well. Even though lesbians earn college degrees at a higher rate than do heterosexual women, most lesbians do not have a college degree, and women without college degrees tend to enter traditionally female occupations, where unionization rates are low and benefits and prestige are in short supply. When women work in occupations that have been male-dominated, they usually have positions low in the hierarchy. Overall, women continue to receive significantly less pay than men. In these respects, lesbians are no better off than heterosexual women, even though they may have more energy for work.

Homophobia is an additional part of lesbians' economic vulnerability. The decision to "come out" at work must be a careful one, depending on the likely response of coworkers and supervisors, and on the political climate. On the one hand, like other women, lesbians seek out social relations with their coworkers; on the other, honest and open friendships are impossible if they cannot share the details of their lives.

The more "professional" the occupation, the more socializing is usually required on the job. Yet the risk of coming out is even greater for lesbians in professional occupations, particularly for those who work in traditionally male occupations. Some traditionally female professions, such as teaching, nursing, and social work, involve work with children; lesbians in such professions feel great social and political pressure not to come out.

Beth Schneider's research on lesbians and work indicates that lesbians tend to be open about their sexual identity when their workplace is small or has a predominance of women, when most of their work friends are women, when they have a female boss or supervisor, when they have little supervisory responsibility, and when their work does not involve children. High-income professional lesbians are likely to be closeted.[25] In Hidalgo's study, 99 percent of the Puerto Rican lesbians in her sample who were active in professional organizations were closeted and felt their coming out would hurt them professionally; these women were predominantly members of the human services professions—social workers, nurses, teachers, lawyers, psychologists, and medical doctors.[26] (These findings are consistent with research on gay men, which shows that economic success frequently seems to require denying one's homosexuality; high-status gay males are less open than are low-status gay males.)[27]

So, while lesbians as a group may be distinctively prepared for the paid labor force and may have a greater commitment to their work than women in general, if they are honest about their sexual identity they likely will not be given what is due to them on the basis of their work or productivity. Because of the likelihood of this injustice, many lesbians keep this basic part of their identity secret.

This contradiction is one many lesbians live with, but at great price. Schneider found that lesbians who remain closeted at work are more concerned about losing their jobs than open lesbians. In addition, closeted lesbians are more concerned about losing their friends, harming their relationships with their parents, and harming their lovers' careers or child custody status. The closet promotes a sense of powerlessness, strain, and anxiety.[28]

The decision to come out must be a calculated one. Job discrimination against gays and lesbians has been the rule rather than the exception. The Supreme Court has yet to rule on the merits of cases involving equal job protection to lesbians and gay men under the law, and in the absence of leadership from the high court, judges in the lower courts have made decisions based primarily on their own assessments of the morality of homosexual behavior. Segments of the private sector, particularly some large corporations, have implemented antidiscriminatory hiring policies, but because the larger culture is still divided about the acceptability of lesbian and gay relationships, the Supreme Court probably will not require all workplaces to do so. Grand constitutional decisions, as in the definitive desegregation and abortion cases, typically follow evolving public mores.[29]

Consequently, lesbians have a well-grounded fear that if they come out at work they will lose their jobs. Between 50 and 75 percent of lesbians fear losing their jobs, and many who do not feel this threat are either self-employed, working in feminist agencies, or working in a small number of occupations in which lesbianism is tolerated.[30] Nearly one-quarter of lesbians report actual instances of formal or informal job discrimination, including not being hired for a job or being fired from a job solely because they were lesbian.[31] Behind these figures are actions many lesbians take to cope with the fear of discrimination, including staying closeted, self-employment, and job tracking, or choosing a job because there is evidence one will not lose it by being discovered to be lesbian. For many women, lesbian identity requires great defensive effort.

Other aspects of economic discrimination against lesbians are more subtle. For example, Barbara Sang notes that homosexual couples cannot benefit from discounts in transportation or from memberships that come with family status. Women tend to know less about the ways of investing the money they earn, and usually there is less money to invest. Many lesbian couples may be afraid to pool their assets for fear of the relationship's breaking up and thus "double spend" on major investments, and a choice to maintain separate residences to avoid being known as living with another woman means the couple cannot benefit from sharing expenses. All these factors can lower a lesbian couple's standard of living and restrict their economic mobility, yet they are not immediately obvious to people who enjoy heterosexual privilege.[32]

Morality, Discrimination, and Public Policy

Discrimination against lesbian women solely because of their sexual orientation is wrong for the same reasons it is wrong to discriminate against any group: because it offends justice, because it deprives them of what they need to fulfill their own life plans, and because it undermines their dignity and the respect they deserve. It offends justice according to work, need, and merit. Societal discrimination against lesbian and gay persons perpetrated through violation of their bodily integrity, improper jailing, gay bashing, and refusal of their right to sexual expression denies them justice according to what the law provides other citizens.

Those who deny that it is wrong to discriminate against lesbian and gay persons maintain that gay people do not deserve equal protection under the law because lesbians and gay men willfully lead an immoral life, flaunting religious law, and because they have through social influence the capacity to directly or indirectly harm others, particularly children.

However, I will argue that the rationales for depriving lesbians and gay men of protections for private consensual sex, civil rights, and family integrity are seriously flawed. I see no moral basis for policies that undermine lesbians' rights to bodily integrity and life plans.

The public policies needed to allow equal participation of lesbian women in the economy include all those policies discussed in previous chapters relating to childbearing and child rearing, sexual harassment, and domestic violence, because lesbians are women. In addition, efforts must be made to allow lesbians equal participation in society without denying their identities as "women-identified women," and these policies would also protect gay men and bisexuals.

Anti-sodomy laws, where they exist, provide the edifice upon which much of the other discrimination against lesbians and gay men rests.[33] In twenty-one states of the United States, same-sex sexual behavior is illegal. Twenty-nine states and the District of Columbia, on the other hand, have decriminalized lesbian and gay male sex acts.[34]

In 1986, the United States Supreme Court upheld the constitutionality of the state of Georgia's sodomy statute. The majority opinion stated that "proscriptions against [homosexual] conduct have ancient roots." A concurring opinion held that "condemnation of those practices is firmly rooted in Judeo-Christian moral and ethical standards." A dissenting opinion objected to the petitioner's invocation of Leviticus and Romans and the assertion that traditional Judeo-Christian values proscribe homosexual conduct.[35] Clearly the Hebrew Scriptures and the New Testament are still operating as justificatory sources in public proscriptions against homosexual actions and identity.

This particular Supreme Court opinion was a response to *Bowers v. Hardwick*. Early one morning in Atlanta in 1982, a policeman knocked at a door and asked for Michael Hardwick. The roommate didn't know if Michael was in, but pointed down the hall to his room. Through a slit in the door, the officer could see Hardwick engaging in consensual gay sex; he entered the room and arrested Michael and his partner. The Supreme Court, using the above reasoning, ruled that Georgia may jail Hardwick for ten years for lovemaking in the privacy of his home, in other words, that privacy rights do not protect gay sex in Georgia.[36] Clearly, the protection of privacy rights for lesbian women and gay men is fundamental to their efforts to plan their lives and protect their persons; decriminalizing consensual gay sex is a component of guarantees to autonomy, the freedom to be responsible.

The second important policy arena for protection of lesbians as women-identified women is that of civil rights. Civil rights for lesbian women and gay men include protection from discrimination based on sexual orientation in public employment, public accommodations, private employment, education, housing, credit, and union practices. Civil rights laws have been passed in some states by their legislatures and signed by their governors, passed in other states through executive order, passed by cities and counties as ordinances, and in cities and counties by council or mayoral proclamations banning discrimination in public employment. In some cases discrimination in all areas is prohibited; in some only one or some other number of these civil rights is protected.

As of 1994, only eighteen states and approximately 130 cities and counties offer protection for public employees against discrimination on the basis of sexual orientation.[37] Some of these states, cities, and counties also protect other civil rights.[38]

The bases for supporting the specific protection of civil rights for gay people—or for opposing them—are related to the overall perspective one holds regarding lesbian and gay identity.

Because Kinsey documented that large numbers of men and

women had engaged in homosexual activity during adolescence and throughout adulthood, he refused to view homosexuality as pathological.[39] The lifting of laws prohibiting adult consensual homosexual sex is consistent with Kinsey's view that there are no homosexual or lesbian people, only homosexual or lesbian acts, which anyone can and many do enjoy.[40] The political implication of such a view is that civil rights for lesbians and gay men should be protected because lesbian women and gay men are *us*. Any one person can experience a predominant sexual identity that undergoes a major shift, or a vacillating sexual identity. There is no them *versus* us, and civil rights that protect heterosexually behaving people should be extended to all people regardless of sexual identity, since one day such laws could protect you.

Among the tendencies in feminist thought, at least one, a stream of cultural feminism, challenges this view of lesbian identity.[41] In this perspective, lesbianism is a political choice. Lesbianism has always been political resistance to patriarchal control, because lesbians are outside the society structured by men for men. From this perspective, every woman could be a lesbian if she so chose; there is no such thing as "sexual orientation"; we all have the potential to be anything, sexually.[42] In this view, the incidence rate of lesbian identity is potentially 100 percent.

This cultural feminist perspective on lesbianism represents a challenge to the dominant paradigm that sexuality and sexual behavior belong to a private and personal sphere; and lesbianism as a challenge to the whole patriarchal society is not simply a search for the private, "true self" which when accepted can result in self-actualization, self-fulfillment, and personal happiness. Cultural feminism nevertheless supports civil rights for gay men and lesbian women because such social policy would provide protection from police and other external coercion and allow some breathing space for political activity.

Representing yet another point of view, researchers Frederick Whitam and Robin Mathy contend that homosexual orientation is biologically derived and immutable, appearing in all societies at about the same rate (5 percent of the male population) and characterized by similar elements in different societies in all historical periods. Homosexuals' civil rights need protection, therefore, because gay people are a true minority. That is, they are a disadvantaged group, excluded from full participation in society, held in low esteem, and often the objects of suspicion, contempt, hatred, and violence. Membership in this group is involuntary, as individuals are born into it, according to this view, and gay men and lesbian women are self-conscious groups, with a history, values, and beliefs, and see themselves and are treated as a "people apart."[43] This understanding of gay and lesbian identity is very different from the perspective that individuals are not by and large born gay or lesbian, but rather experiment in various ways with sexual behaviors and relationships before stepping into an identity that then becomes stable over time (before, perhaps, shifting again).

Perhaps the strongest voices arguing that gay men and lesbians should not be treated equally by society have been those of conservative members of the Roman Catholic, Protestant, Jewish, and Muslim communities. Among Christians there is a direct relationship between church attendance, orthodoxy, devotion, fundamentalism, and disapproval of homosexuality.[44] Traditionally religious people view gay rights legislation as part of a general strategy to promote homosexual acts as a normal variant of human behavior and homosexuality as an alternative lifestyle. They resist that goal because they believe that homosexual acts are morally wrong and should not be given either protection or acceptance.

Enrique Rueda, of the Free Congress Research and Education Foundation, represents such a view:

> The acceptance of homosexual behavior as normal implies
> not only the willingness to engage in social intercourse
> with individuals known or suspected to be homosexual,
> but the positive acknowledgment that when these individu-
> als seek relief from their sexual urges, they do so without
> violating their own nature or the relationships demanded
> by the ontic [actual, real] structure of their sexuality. The
> acceptance of homosexuality as an alternative lifestyle
> implies the extension of American cultural pluralism to
> areas that have been considered manifestations of deprav-
> ity, emotional disorders and / or sociopathic personalities.[45]

What this religious opposition to gay rights perceives to be at stake is nothing less than the "traditional values" of American society, the structure of the family, and basic concepts of sex as a core element in human personality. Why, in this view, grant civil rights to people who represent such a cosmic threat?—far from being discriminated against, lesbians and gay men have been liberally tolerated far too long.

This religious opposition to civil rights demands a religious response. The liberal churches have not effectively made a case for gay and lesbian civil rights because they themselves have been riven by controversy over the acceptability of homosexual relations, the morality of blessing gay and lesbian unions, and the ordination of gay and lesbian people to the ministry of the word and sacrament.

Both sides of the debate have attempted to draw on the Christian Bible as a justification for their arguments, despite the fact that appeals to Scripture as *the* authority for moral argument are not particularly effective in debate with nonbelievers. No consensus is emerging as to how the Bible should be used to reflect on the morality of homosexual relations, but I believe that the New Testament does not prohibit sexual acts.

I lean heavily on the biblical scholarship of Bill Countryman, who holds the biblical treatment of sexual ethics is controlled by concerns about purity and protection of property.[46] Women do not fare well with regard to either concern, as women's normal if not routine menstrual and postpartum fluids are seen as "polluting," and women as wives and daughters are seen as property. Homosexual acts (the Bible does not discuss "sexual orientation," which is a modern cultural construct) are prohibited as an offense against purity, as the only prohibition against male-with-male sexual acts in the Hebrew Scriptures appears in the Holiness Code (Leviticus 17–26), where the rules about how to avoid defilement are spelled out. The Holiness Code concerns the slaughter of animals and disposition of blood, prohibition of intercourse during the menstrual period, prohibitions of priests with blemishes from officiating in the capacity of priest, prohibitions against incest, and the impurity of people with leprosy, among other things. According to Countryman, purity law is oriented around the principles that every individual should be a complete and self-contained specimen of its kind (and therefore not be blemished) and that there not be mixing of kinds. The reason for the condemnation of male homosexual acts is that one of the men fulfills the "female" role, and is therefore unclean because he is a combination of kinds.[47] In addition, according to biblical scholar Victor Furnish, the receiving partner's maleness has been compromised and he is no longer an unblemished specimen.[48] The prohibition against male-with-male sexual acts is therefore dependent upon the devaluation of women.

This purity code as found in Torah probably reached its final form by the fifth century B.C.E., and the New Testament or Second Testament documents date from half a millennium later. The four evangelists reject physical purity as a necessary condition for relationship to God. The concern for purity that remains in the Gospels relates to purity of intentions and motivation, concern for whether persons by their thoughts and actions intend harm or are motivated by care and compassion. Sexual acts are thereby not governed by concerns of physical contagion. Only intent to harm renders a sexual act impure.[49]

Paul used the term "uncleanness" as an equivalent for greed, referring to the private vice of lust and the social vice of wanting to have more than another or what rightfully belongs to another.[50] Romans 1:18–32 is the passage that is usually interpreted as Paul's clearest statement that homosexual acts are sin. However, Countryman finds that "while Paul wrote of homosexual acts as being unclean, dishonorable, improper, and over against nature, he did not call them sin. He treated homosexual behavior as an integral if unpleasingly dirty aspect of Gentile culture."[51] Such behavior was visited upon the Gentiles as a fair return for their sins of idolatry and social disruption. But, like the writers of the Gospels, Paul refrained from identifying physical impurity with sin, and rejected physical purity as a prerequisite of salvation or of membership in the Christian community.

Thus the New Testament did not justify any sexual rule by appeal to physical purity, and the Christian is free to be repelled by or to practice her or his own purity code in relation to masturbation, nonvaginal heterosexual intercourse, homosexual acts, or erotic art and literature. Like all sexual acts, these may be genuinely wrong where they involve an offense against equality of women and men, or a substitution of sex for the reign of justice as the goal of human existence.[52] But the New Testament does not provide authority for proscriptions against homosexual acts, or by extension, homosexual identity, in and of themselves.

The use of Scripture to develop moral arguments for today is fraught with difficulty. The most notable problem is the difficulty of drawing a "dynamic analogy" between the world the texts address and the world of contemporary readers.[53] Only when we understand the animating vision compelling the authors of the biblical texts can we apply their lessons to our own day. The biblical scholars I lean on in this work are authoritative for me because they have convinced me that this vision is one of community marked by protection for the vulnerable, sharing risks and benefits of life together, and human responsibility for the quality of economic relations as constitutive of faithful living. This vision provides an ethical criterion for contemporary readers, and such a criterion is always necessary for the interpretation and application of the Bible.[54]

This vision is sometimes obscured because some parts of the texts were also intended to provide or justify special privileges for various elites, such as the priests or the court of David (reflecting motives not unlike the motivations of some of today's social critics, including some religious leaders). However, the animating vision of community is never totally buried even in these texts, and is particularly illustrated by the jubilee mandates as discussed in Chapter 1. So I accept the portions of the Holiness Code that are motivated by a vision of how to share the risks and benefits of life together in society, and how to ensure that people can always provide for themselves and their families. And I reject other portions that are motivated by adherence to a pollution/purity code or assume the view that some persons are the property of others.

All the hierarchical relationships of unaccountable social and familial power that developed in the course of building the community in biblical times were criticized by the prophets, including Jesus of Nazareth, who attempted to restore the animating vision in his day. The dynamic analogy that we need to draw concerns how to identify those structural and religious practices that prevent the world of today from egalitarian sharing of both risks and securities of life together on planet Earth. I believe cultural proscriptions against lesbian and gay identities prevent such egalitarian sharing.

Clearly, some biblical scholars take a very different view of the biblical warrants regarding sexual ethics.[55] But I have yet to find a biblically based argument against homosexuality that does not rest on the purity code, although most scholarship at the same time challenges the purity code as a requirement for inclusion in Christian community, challenges "property" as the rubric governing male-female relations, and acknowledges that the effort to use Scripture in moral argument requires drawing dynamic analogy with the world of the text rather than a mechanical transference of the words to issues of our time. I believe we should move beyond both purity and property as groundings for our sexual ethics, to justice as right relationship, with all that might involve.

The third arena of public policy change concerns family law. Family law is of great consequence for the economic stability of lesbians and gay men. Family law includes issues such as marriage, child custody, child visitation rights, adoptions, and financial support after separation. In particular, the extension of family law to protect the rights of people in lesbian and gay committed partnerships to raise their own children is contingent upon the prior decriminalization of private, consensual sexual conduct by adults of the same sex. As it is, the legal treatment of issues related to lesbians and gay men is permeated with prejudicial attitudes regarding the morality of homosexual acts. The American legal system has only recently, in some specific jurisdictions, begun to accept the notion that a good parent also may be homosexual.[56] "It is not a written law that because you're a lesbian you should have your children taken away—it is an assumption made by all the judges, or has been."[57]

At least three million lesbians and gay men are parents of children. Estimates of the number of children of gay or lesbian parents range from 6 million to 14 million.[58] Most of these children are the product of a heterosexual relationship and/or marriage, but increasing numbers of lesbians and gay men are having children outside of marriage also, through donor insemination, adoption, foster care, and co-parenting.

The most commonly litigated conflict in the area of lesbian and gay rights is over child custody and visitation when a marriage dissolves and one parent is homosexual.[59] Because legal standards for determining the best interests of the children are vague, they are open to interpretation, and frequently judges have presumed against gay and lesbian parents.

Judge Donna Hitchens traces four themes that recur in judicial decisions involving a homosexual parent.[60] First is a concern that a child raised in a lesbian or gay household will be stigmatized, if not now, then certainly in time. Even when there is no evidence of problems for a child in a lesbian or gay home, judges, probation officers, and psychiatrists assume trouble will begin in the future and that the child is better off in a heterosexual household. The second recurring theme is a fear that children raised by gay or lesbian parents will grow up to be homosexual or in some way evidence sociopathology. There is no evidence that homosexuality is "catching" from adult role models.[61] In fact, there is an adage among lesbian mothers that the surest guarantee that children will grow up heterosexual is their living with a lesbian mother.

The third theme is an unquestioning assumption that given a choice between a heterosexual and a homosexual home environment, the heterosexual environment is prima facie better for the child. This assumption is never buttressed by evidence, but is probably a corollary to the first two themes.

The fourth theme is that custody decisions are always subject to renegotiation. Although the courts generally treat the parent-child relationship with deference, they are also duty-bound to intervene for the protection of the child. The court may conclude that a child's welfare requires removal from the custody of a homosexual parent. Most custody struggles occur at the dissolution of a marriage, but custody decisions can be reopened at any time, whether by an estranged spouse, a relative who learns of the custodial parent's homosexuality, or even by a representative of a social service agency. The majority of custody cases involving homosexual parents concern lesbian mothers. Consequently, lesbian mothers live with a constant fear that custody may be taken from them.

Are the concerns of judges justified? Most of the empirical research on the development of children with lesbian or gay parents has been conducted since 1970, stimulated by the phenomenon of openly gay or lesbian parents seeking to retain their parental role. Researchers have found that concerns about the psychological health and development of children of gay and lesbian parents are not justified. There are no significant differences in sexual identity, self-concept, moral judgment, or intelligence between children of lesbian or gay parents and children of heterosexual parents. Children of lesbian and gay parents have normal relationships with peers and their relationships with adults of both sexes are also satisfactory. Home environments provided by gay and lesbian parents are as likely as those provided by heterosexual parents to support and enable children's psychosocial growth. Existing research evidence provides no justification for the denial of parental rights and responsibilities to lesbians and gay men on the basis of their sexual orientation.[62]

The constant fear of a custody challenge, plus the economic and emotional stress of involvement with the court, are significant factors in the lives of lesbian mothers. Some advocacy organizations have helped lesbians who have refused to keep their sexual identities secret and at the same time refused to concede their parental rights. Because of this support, lesbian mother cases and gay father visitation cases are increasingly successful in the courts. But the state of the law regarding family life will be fair only when it removes homosexuality as a relevant factor per se in judicial decisions, making room for the establishment of criteria for the well-being of the family and children that are equally applicable to heterosexual and homosexual committed unions.

Judicial reforms to guarantee freedom from antigay discrimination in family conflicts, child custody, job hiring and firing, and private consensual sex among adults are incremental reforms that serve two purposes. One is to extend the legal protection of the courts to lesbian and gay people who seek equal treatment without regard to their sexual orientation. This is an appeal to equal protection of the law as a measure of justice. It would mean people cannot be refused a job or fired from one, be prevented from playing a parental role, or be ignored after being assaulted, solely because of their sexual orientation.

The second purpose is to neutralize the negative effect of the law in discriminating against lesbians and gay men. No longer would a policeman be permitted to invade private quarters to arrest those engaged in consensual adult sex. Constitutional principles have been evaded by the courts over the years in a systematic sanctioning of the oppression of homosexual people. The law has been a tool of the larger society's fear and hatred of homosexual people and behavior, rather than the critical vantage point for the deliberation of the merits of positions in conflict, as it pretends.[63]

Perhaps by virtue of being "outlaw" women, according to some psychologists, lesbians have had to develop personality qualities that traditionally have been the domain of males but are required for autonomy, community building, and the development of a life plan—qualities such as independence, self-determination, self-confidence, competence, and assertiveness. It is not clear whether lesbians are initially more independent and inner-directed than heterosexual women or develop these qualities as a reaction to societal pressure.[64] So, while the force of stigma is great, lesbians are finding ways to exert countervailing energy to develop economic independence and social freedom from a male supremacist culture. Freedom from sexual harassment in the workplace, access to quality child care and to parental leave, and protection by the police and the courts in the event of domestic violence are all pieces of the social support lesbian women need in order to develop economic independence as *women*. In addition, that economic independence must be buttressed by protection of civil rights, including rights to family participation, that will protect them as women-identified women, and will protect gay men as well.

chapter six

Sexual Ethics

A T THE BEGINNING of this book, I claimed that women's experiences of sexuality compromise our access to the economy in a different way than is true for men. By now it should be clear that this claim really refers to the definition of women as sexual persons by social tradition and to a system of male dominance: women as mothers, women as conquered or sexually exploited at work, women as sexual property, and women without men as outsiders. All these treatments of women have economic causes and consequences, and, most important for the moral argument, they require women to contribute more to the economy and society than they receive in return from the economy. If I am right, then sexual ethics have economic significance when and because they contain gender expectations. Therefore, it could well be said that sexual ethics is a piece of the constructive task in economic ethics. Is there a sexual ethic that challenges women's secondary and derivative economic status and is committed to women's well-being in all ways?

Beverly Harrison, James Nelson, Margaret Farley, and other scholars have spent the past two decades reflecting on questions of sexual morality in ways that take seriously the effects of sexism as a power dynamic in any sexual relation. Theirs is a body of work that I call "progressive sexual ethics." Without representing the whole of each of their writings, I will synthesize here the work of Harrison, Nelson, and Farley as it contributes to the progressive sexual ethic, which can be characterized by six principles:

1. Our personal sexuality is to be celebrated, not deprecated.
2. Mutuality, not ownership or control, should be the major moral norm for sexual communication.
3. The principle of bodily integrity should govern the practice of touching another or responding to another's touch.
4. Sex-role fluidity is preferable to rigidity, which impedes mature interpersonal relations.
5. The many kinds of sexual communication between people who care for each other, consistent with the requirements of mutuality, should be recognized and honored. A single sex ethic should govern all sexual relations, whether they be heterosexual or homosexual.
6. To buttress the capacity of women to develop and live by freely chosen life plans, social policy should provide basic material supports for procreative choice.

While these principles are formulated and justified by the authors in ways that can be affirmed or argued with by all people regardless of religious affiliation or lack of it, they are also justified theologically in biblical justice as right relationship, discussed in Chapter 1. Biblical justice is the personality of God / ess, who defends the vulnerable. Justice is also the requirement for participation in the covenants and it exacts demands on interpersonal and social relations. It requires fidelity to the demands of a relationship, recognizing that different relationships carry different demands, in order to preserve wholeness of the community and the dignity and integrity of the persons in the relationship.

Basic Principles of Sexual Ethics

Let's explore each principle in turn. The first is that *our personal sexuality is to be celebrated rather than deprecated*, because our sexuality is at the core of who we are, the grounding of our capacity to communicate with and care for others, and, finally, the center of our capacity to love justice and act in solidarity with the victims of injustice.[1] There is a direct relationship between the acceptance of our personal sexuality and our capacity to make just social relationships. Why? Because while acceptance of our sexuality does not require that we act on all our sexual desires, if we cannot acknowledge our feelings we have difficulty identifying them and can spend a great deal of energy denying they exist. Such denial truncates our capacity for empathy with others, which is necessary to want justice for them.[2] Guilt drains moral sensitivity.[3]

Explicit sexuality pervades our culture today because it is the medium used to sell products. This is not the sexuality that grounds our capacity to communicate with and care for others, though; this explicit sexuality is "canned." Its message is that women are at our core pleasured only when we are serving the sexual needs of men. This fixation on female submissive sexuality, and on genital sexuality, is not what is meant by saying our sexuality is to be celebrated. More fittingly, we can appropriate the work of the Boston Women's Health Book Collective, who made available a phrase that opens another meaning of sexuality, and this is that we are "our bodies, ourselves." Our power of self-determination as moral agents arises with our exercise of a freedom to understand, control, and direct our own sexuality.[4] This view precludes the familiar popular ideal of romance, which involves seduction and conquest on the male side and feminine passivity and denial of pleasure on the other. However, it also opposes the belief that sexuality is the root of all evil. For it is only after celebrating sexuality that we can put it in its place.[5]

The principle of celebrating our sexuality sustains the personal autonomy of each of us, not in the sense that each of us is an isolated individual whose sexuality is our own individual property, but rather in the sense that each of us is a moral agent only when we are acting out of who we are in our body selves. The concept of moral agency has two dimensions. One who is moving into their moral agency is moving away from being an object of history toward being a subject of history, away from being powerless and toward expressing personal and / or political power. Moral agents in this first sense are persons who are reflective about the moral dimensions of the situations they find themselves in and about their actions, and see themselves as having a degree of power and autonomy out of which to make decisions. This personal and political power is embodied—experienced intellectually, emotionally, and physically.

The second dimension of moral agency is willingness to accept moral responsibility for our behavior. We *are* morally responsible when we knowingly and willingly cause something to happen or fail to respond when we could. We are not morally responsible for actions that are impossible to perform, or for things we do not know how to do, nor for things we know nothing about and could not be expected to know about. Moral responsibility in this sense is about accountability for things done or undone, whether we wish to be held accountable or not.

Since our bodies possess ways of knowing morally, when we are cut off from body awareness and bodily integrity, our capacity to know the moral dimensions of a situation is impeded. In such circumstances we may fail to respond appropriately, and in this sense be irresponsible or unresponsive. In recognizing that our bodies can be a source of knowing morally, we claim an expanded view of ourselves as capable of being sensitive to moral meanings. We may not listen well enough or understand clearly *what* we know morally, but our bodies are sources of moral knowledge.

Recognizing the body as a source of knowledge does not preclude other sources of knowledge, such as rationality, disinterestedness, or detachment. Such habits of mind allow us to listen to other people in conversation or in our moral imaginations, to understand what it would be like to be in someone else's shoes. The point is to heal the mind / body split, rather than line up behind one or the other.

Sexual communication and sexual intimacy have the power to sustain human dignity. Therefore, sexuality is not dirty or wrong, or something to be repressed or too tightly controlled. But the view of sex as dirty is an integral part of an anti-body, antinature dualism which has a powerful hold in Western tradition. This dualism has promoted pervasive hostility to women, evident in the view that females lack some ingredient, for instance rationality, that is necessary for the full range of ideal human functioning. As a result, many women absorb the message that things are safer when men are "in charge." This antisexual, anti-body, antinatural dualism is an aspect of the ideology of control developed in pa-triarchal social systems to keep women in secondary status.[6]

The anti-body dualism that sustains the male/female dualism also sustains white supremacy, for again, whites define men and women of color as more natural, controlled by feelings, more physical and less rational than they. Anti-body dualism serves as an ideology to justify dominate/subordinate relationships, an ideology to explain why the dominant class and race is on top, and should stay there.

Beverly Harrison explains the positive view of sexuality con-tained in the progressive sexual ethic when she says,

> Our sexuality is the deepest, most intense dimension of our interaction with the world and because it is, it really is a key to the quality and integrity of our over-all spirituality. Literally, our [body-space] is the ground of our person-hood, and is the means by which we communicate the power of our presence to and with others. How we deal with our own body-space and how we relate to others' [body-space] provides the deepest paradigm for our moral relations to the world.[7]

One of the implications of such a view is that touch is not mor-ally inferior to other modes of communication. The intensity of touch may warrant our tender use of its power, but not its com-pulsive control.[8]

The second principle is that *mutuality is a major moral norm for sexual communication.* How are we to recognize mutuality? One of its characteristics is equal power in a relationship. This may be difficult to measure at any particular time, particularly since there are many dimensions of personal and social power, all of which are constantly shifting in significance within any rela-tionship. In addition, even an unequal relationship will often *feel* mutual to the one who expresses more power in it. Yet however hard to measure, this value is real, and it challenges the morality of the traditional concept of marriage, in which two persons be-come one and that one is the husband. Harrison says she shudders

> to think how many times in my years of theological study I came upon a male theologian writing that we should not

confuse real, Christian love with 'mere mutuality.' One senses that persons who can think this way have yet to experience the power of love as the real pleasure of mutual vulnerability, the experience of truly being cared for or of actively caring for another. Mutual love is love in its deepest radicality.[9]

A second measure of mutuality, as Margaret Farley articulates it, is that both persons in a mutual relationship are active and passive, giving and receiving, and that the relationship is neither authoritarian nor hierarchical. While equality is the minimal *requirement* of justice, mutuality is the *goal* of justice.[10] This reciprocity appears in Harrison's work when she defines radical mutuality as the simultaneous acknowledgment of vulnerability to and need of another and the recognition of one's own power to give pleasure and call forth another's power of affirmation.

Respect for one's own and the other's autonomy is a component of mutuality. Adults who abuse children sexually often rationalize their actions, saying the child is seductive and receives mutual pleasure. In the face of such evidence of adults who lack self-control, these authors answer that mutuality rejects as inappropriate *all* sexual relations characterized by inequities of power. This ethic is much stronger than "It's okay as long as nobody gets hurt," which is a negative standard. Rather, an ethic of mutuality insists that people's sense of self-worth and autonomy should be enhanced by any sexual encounter. Sex between adults and children is wrong because children are needy, vulnerable, and psychologically dependent. Sex between doctors and patients, clergy and parishioners, professors and students, supervisors and supervisees is wrong because the powerful member in these relationships holds control over something the other needs. This norm also rules out high-pressure seduction and any other sexual relationships or acts based upon manipulation of one person at the expense of another. But this ethic does not condemn any sexual act or sexual relationship of equality expressed in a way consistent with mutuality, defined as equal power in a relationship, reciprocity, and respect for the autonomy of the other.[11]

The third principle of the progressive sexual ethic is a corollary to the first two: *the principle of bodily self-determination or bodily integrity must be respected*. This principle applies to all relationships and is at stake in a wide range of situations—when slavery exists, when patients do not have the opportunity to give informed consent to a medical procedure, during hazing. Violation of the principle of bodily integrity violates the autonomy of the moral agent. As Harrison states, "Our bodies *are* ourselves, and they *should* be ours, unmediated by others' power to determine, control, manipulate, or seduce."[12] The integrity of the body self is fundamental to the expression of moral freedom and responsibility. Unless we can control what happens to our bodies— or have the freedom to choose our responses to threats such as disease, over which no one has control—we lack the very basis for morally responsible behavior.

Even a casual touch, if unwanted, can violate the bodily integrity of the person touched. Bosses tend to touch employees, men to touch women, adults to touch younger people, and white people to touch people of other colors. In this way the privileged assume access to the other's body self; this is a mechanism for social control. Clearly, no one should "celebrate" touch and sexuality by violating the principles of mutuality and respect for bodily self-determination.

The fourth principle promotes *sex-role fluidity, or the practice of behaving in both "feminine" and "masculine" ways*. It's opposite, sex-role rigidity, is the practice of limiting one's behavior to what is feminine if you are female, or masculine if you are male. Rigid sex-roles inappropriately limit behavior, rather than encouraging appropriate responses to a given situation. Farley has focused on this issue:

> What differences there are between women and men are not differences which justify gender-specific variations in a right to education, to work, to access to occupational spheres, to participation in political life, to just wages, to share in the burdens and responsibilities of family, society, and church. History clearly shows that efforts to restrict social roles on the basis of sex inevitably lead to inequities, to circumscription of persons in a way that limits the possibilities of growth in human and Christian life.[13]

Religious traditions can be the most vigorous promoters of sex-role rigidity. We need only to reflect on the extent to which the churches have taught that the home and family is the central place for Christian labor when it is the labor of women. Women's task has been to prepare children to move beyond the home and family and to provide support for men when they come home; but for men, the family is only a refuge, as men's real and important work is in the public arena. In the progressive sexual ethic the family is indeed a place for labor—for both men and women—just as the public sphere is.[14]

Additionally, sex roles have been given a religious cast when the thinkers of the church, in coming to conclusions about differences between women and men, have extrapolated from biological (or "physical") data. Even if it were logical to derive rules for human behavior from the physics of heterosexual sex, claims Farley, rigid sex-roles would not be the correct result:

> To fail to see all the ways in which, even at a physical level, men's bodies receive, encircle, embrace, and all the ways women's bodies are active, giving, penetrating, is to undermine from the start any possibility of growing insight into patterns of mutuality in relationships between persons.[15]

Sex-role fluidity means that people behave in ways appropriate to the situation, rather than in a preset fashion. This doubles the range of appropriate behavior for all women and men, and thus expands the arena of what we can immediately grasp as the meaning of moral autonomy. Since moral autonomy is the freedom to be responsible, sex-role fluidity enlarges our conceptions of how to exercise that responsibility. And when sex roles are no longer rigid, we as women will not feel anxious about our femininity when we participate well in situations requiring competence and leadership, including when we give direction about what pleasures us. Similarly, men will not feel anxious about their masculinity when they participate well in situations requiring equality, listening, and empathy. Sex-role fluidity enhances the possibility of mutuality.

The fifth principle of the progressive sexual ethic supports *a single sex ethic governing all sexual relations*. There are two issues here. The first is that there is a wide range of sexual expression between adults, including eye contact, touching, comforting, caressing, massaging to stimulation, and orgasm. Each interpersonal relation has an appropriate range of sexual expression, and most relationships have a very small range, toward the early end of this list, as they are not intended to be "romantic." James Nelson claims that our aim should be to choose a range of sexual expression which is appropriate to the level of commitment present in a relationship, whether the relationship be male / female or same-sex.[16] The point is to relate our body selves in a mutually enhancing and pleasuring way, consistent with the right to bodily integrity, and that may include genital expression but it may not. Our reflective attention to the *various* ways we relate sexually to men and to women, some involving pleasurable conversation, others emotional support, and still others the promise of body contact, should reveal the wide range of heterosexual and homosexual relations all of us are already sustaining. In addition, we can be attentive to the satisfactions of relationships at whatever range of sexual expression, as opposed to evaluating each one in terms of whether it will lead to genital sexual expression or is satisfying only in those terms.

The second issue present in this principle is the movement toward seeking a single sex ethic for homosexual, bisexual, and heterosexual relations, and toward viewing sexual expression as communication, or human relationship, not as fundamentally a means to procreation.[17] The decision to bring forth new life is certainly a moral one, with its own concerns for how we can sustain the personhood of the new human being and the consequences of that decision for everyone else affected. But the decision to be sexually active with another is (with the responsible use of effective contraceptives if heterosexual, and the willingness to obtain an early abortion if contraception fails) potentially quite a different moral decision. The authors whose work I am relying on here, in calling for a single sex ethic, wish to replace procreation as the purpose of sexual relations. In doing so, they challenge a central aspect of traditional sexual ethics. Farley describes the common traditional Christian belief that sexual desire is inherently selfish because it is seen as a desire for pleasure for its own sake, which also sees sexual desire as a cause of disorder in the emotional and spiritual life of persons because it cannot be contolled by reason in the same way that other basic needs and drives can be controlled. For those who take this view, the rational good of pro-creation is the only justification for sexual activity.[18]

The authors of the progressive sexual ethic challenge directly or by implication every component of this view of sexual desire, and Farley maintains that even within Roman Catholic ethics there are grounds for rejecting this tradition. Sexual desire is not inherently selfish, even if it relishes pleasure for its own sake, for the heights of sexual pleasure are experienced mutually. Sexual desire is not a cause of emotional or spiritual disorder in that it is not controlled by reason, for all persons are accountable for their *actions*. And procreation can rarely, in the span of a person's life cycle, be the rational goal or consequence of sexual desire, not in the contemporary world where by our numbers human beings are decreasing the life-support systems of other species and, by extension, our own. With procreation displaced as the purpose of sexual desire, it becomes possible to claim that homosexual relations should be judged by the same standards as heterosexual relations, consistent with the principles of celebration, mutuality, bodily integrity, and so on, and this has implications for the sixth principle.

The sixth principle is that in order to buttress the capacity of women to develop and live by freely-chosen life plans, *social policy should provide basic material supports for procreative choice*. Procreative choice is the right of women to choose to have children, to delay having children, or to forego having children. This choice is ours to responsibly make whether our context includes a committed relationship to a partner or not, though because of the consequences of such a choice we owe it to our partners to involve them in the decision to the degree to which they have given evidence they will be responsible in dealing with its consequences.

Procreative choice includes negative rights, such as the right to not be excluded from the political process, privacy rights, the right to say no to unwanted sexual contact, the right to define ourselves sexually, and the right to say yes to sexual relations that are not geared toward procreation at all but are for the responsible pleasure of it.[19] Procreative choice also requires positive rights, such as access to information about our body selves, to trustworthy contraception and the basic health care to support it, and access to prenatal and postnatal health care, good quality child care, housing, and either basic income or the right to a job.

In this framework, procreative choice is therefore defined much more broadly than as the right to abortion, though access to abortion is certainly included. It also includes the right to have children, which is violated when sterilization is "exchanged" for food with very poor women,[20] and when contraception is forced on women. (Some of the earliest proponents of this broad definition of procreative choice were responding to the apparently genocidal nature of sterilization abuse: a 1970 study of fertility nationwide reported that 20 percent of all black married women had been sterilized, at least 19 percent of all Native American women had been sterilized, and 35 percent of all Puerto Rican women had been sterilized.)[21] Procreative choice also includes the capacity to time births in a manner consistent with the life plans we have chosen.

Given that women today do face abortion decisions, experience coercion in contraception, and live with forced or unneeded sterilization, what kind of sexual ethic would have to be in place to reduce the occurrence of such situations? The progressive sexual ethic would, if the norm, encourage social practices that would protect procreative choice, including procreative responsibility. Misinformation and ambivalence about sex would be less of a problem in a social environment where sexuality was celebrated and mutuality and sex-role fluidity were the norms. Use of contraceptive measures is only consistent under such conditions. Sexual coercion is the antithesis of mutuality and bodily self-determination, as is coerced contraception, abortion, or sterilization. And if we were to take women's body rights seriously, we would either have safer contraception or be less inclined to doubt the moral responsibility of women who face the consequences of failed contraception. This is not to say there would be no moral quandry about the choice for abortion, but it is better that each of us face any quandry knowing we are valued as moral agents, that our bodily integrity is important, and that the outcome has not been predetermined by gender expectations.

Does the progressive sexual ethic justify coitus before marriage? Yes. It also justifies coitus after marriage and when marriage is illegal. It may also justify coitus outside of marriage, though there is a predisposition toward long-term committed relationships in the mutuality norm. Does this ethic assume sexual morality is an individualistic concern, denying the importance of individuals' actions to the whole community? No. All sexual ethics are social ethics, whether acknowledged as such or not, and describe normative expressions of social power.

The following discussion evaluates the progressive sexual ethic in terms of three particular questions. The first question concerns the focus of this book—the impact on women's economic situation. The second and third arise from the historical circumstances of this era, to which any new developments in sexual ethics should be attentive.

Women and Economic Vulnerability

Is the progressive sexual ethic adequate in light of the experiences of economic vulnerability of women who have known childbirth and child rearing, sexual harassment, domestic violence, and / or lesbian relations? Yes, I believe this ethic is quite useful for criticizing economic injustice and envisioning new possibilities. The right to social supports buttressing procreative choice addresses the issue of societal responsibility with regard to child rearing, and the needs of parents for flexible work responsibilities. The principles of mutuality and bodily integrity forbid the coercive or hostile sex characteristic of sexual harassment and domestic violence. The celebration of our sexuality and the affirmation of a single sexual ethic removes the stigma against same-sex relations.

In addition, as a sexual ethic, this body of work represents a genuine alternative to the misogynist understanding of sex as an inherently dominant / subordinate relation, with women assumed to be natural subordinates. It does not focus on the physical structure of sexual acts or the status of those engaged in the acts, but rather on the nature of the relationship in which sexual acts occur and the consequences of those acts. The progressive sexual ethic does not fixate on coitus as the only "real" sexual act, but recognizes that we nourish sexual relations expressed through a range of behaviors. And it recognizes that sexual relations should be accountable to the norms and values we hold in political and other social relationships.[22]

My basic concern about the progressive sexual ethic is rooted in my belief that women need more control over the boundaries of all romantic relationships, particularly early ones and heterosexual, sexually intimate ones. Sexual intimacy still carries a subtext of sex roles in heterosexual relations: the male owns his sexual partner and the female submits to his promise of security as well as his control. In addition, we need to teach our children that sexual intimacy, particularly when it involves coitus, has the power to derail life plans. The demands of a relationship, as well as the risk of pregnancy, have an importance in our setting of goals that is not to be ignored. The six principles of the progressive sexual ethic may not acknowledge clearly enough the power we each hold to sustain or hurt each other through word and touch.

This "defensive" posture does risk hearkening back to the dominant ethic regarding control or "ownership" of sexuality. But, considering the significance of the age of a woman when she gives birth to her first child, the pervasive practice of sexual harassment (some expressions of which begin as amorous), and the ease with which one can get into and the difficulty of getting out of a relationship marked by domestic violence, I believe that a certain wariness is essential. How can we encourage such wariness without undermining the celebration of our sexuality or shutting off the vulnerabilty that is required for mutuality?

Perhaps one key to unlocking this perplexity is conflict. Conflict between people in any relationship need not be a sign of immaturity, poor fit, or a lack of commitment. Conflict can be the way to stop business as usual and begin the process of renegotiating the terms of a relationship, making possible a deepening of the grounds for a history that will be shared. It is a gift to all of us, adolescents included, to be able to use conflict when mutuality is being undermined, sex-roles rigidified, sexuality debased, or self-determination denied. If one partner blocks the renegotiation for which conflict signals the need, that may be grounds for terminating the relationship, but for girls, especially, healthy doses of conflict can have the effect of buttressing identities, identities that make possible the celebration of our sexuality and mutuality in relationship.[23] If one knows how to engage in good, productive conflict in a relationship, one can be less wary of entering one.

My second concern about the progressive sexual ethic is that if it is to become morally binding, as I hope it will, we may need to lift up in a new way some structures of accountability to it. For starters, we would need men and women, but particularly men, to be willing to induce shame as a social control mechanism when this ethic is violated. Men must not give double messages to each other to both be responsible with their power of touch and at the same time to establish their masculinity by "scoring," creating babies, or humiliating women. Women are already held accountable for males' sexual behavior as well as their own, so there may be less of a parallel role for shame with women in this regard. For an ethic to become the operative norm there must be a community of accountability, people who believe, live by, and proclaim norms upholding women's bodily integrity, and costs to those who violate these norms. While the law provides sanctions in some areas, it cannot be effective by itself.

Thirdly, I suggest that we make *the right to a life plan, or project*, a component of this sexual ethic—that is, the right to choose the values that will shape the commitments upon which one takes action, to choose the overall directions one will take to meet one's needs for work, intimacy, and community, and to revise one's plans in light of wisdom gained in living. The right to a life project is a necessary precursor to social policy supporting procreative choice, and without the right to choose if and when to have children, women can have no life plans. The right to a life plan is foreign to many girls, who frequently see their futures sculpted first by their parents, then by their husbands. It is also foreign to many who are poor, who find social forces external to themselves to be more significant than their own intentions in shaping their lives. An incapacity to imagine how one will direct one's life is the result of social patterns as much as individual capability.

The philosophical "law of the most inclusive end," passed into contemporary moral theory through the personalist tradition, is one possible contribution to the effort to emphasize the importance of a life project.[24] It states that "all persons ought to choose a coherent life in which the widest possible range of value is realized." In this perspective, we are asked to choose the values by which we will direct our lives, and choose them in such a way that they are coherent with each other, considering our lives both at any given time and in terms of its whole span. This principle requires that we have a vision of how society can be, and that we be involved in shaping our communities, for individual persons are rarely able to achieve wholeness independently of the communities, local and global, in which we live. Life goals, steadily sought, give rise to a profile of emphasis on certain virtues.[25] We become a certain kind of person as we develop patterns of behavior in seeking our ideals. Choosing is linked to character in this way.

One value of an emphasis on the right to a life plan (or even a duty to have one) is that it provides the goals against which to evaluate consequences and the principles of sexual ethics. That is, when we evaluate possibilities for and make choices about behavior, a life plan gives us something against which to calculate whether we are on track. We are to choose the widest possible range of values to realize, so it's explicit that there is room for revision and redirection of our plans, and rigidity is no virtue.

Another value of the right to a life plan is that it invites us to link individual decisions about sexual relations to wider social structures. In this way, we can come to see that wholeness for many people depends on major social changes. For example, for some people sexual performance or conquest is the only arena available for building self-esteem, hence the value of celebration of sexuality is distorted; not until these persons claim and are granted significant access to the economic and political arenas will they have avenues to build self-esteem consistent with the common good. Nurturing children is a very important activity, but if parenting is the only way in which we as adults can contribute our talents to the community, as it is for women whose work is defined solely in relation to the private sphere, nurturing can become oppressive; in such a context, population stabilization and decrease can only come at the expense of some people's single arena of accomplishment. In another example, homophobia robs people of the right to a life plan, which requires honesty with ourselves and others; but until honesty will not be punished by losing child visitation, custody rights, employment, and / or housing, it cannot be expected. The concept of a life plan both helps us to assess the wholeness of our lives and their trajectories, and requires us to see ourselves as persons in communities that require analysis and ever-changing forms of social accountability.

In the Face of Disease and Death

Are the principles of the progressive sexual ethic useful for people with AIDS or other life-threatening illnesses? The knowledge that one has such a life-threatening disease can challenge one's view of oneself as sexual, one's sense of one's body as having integrity, and one's life plan in its main outlines.

On the face of it, one would not expect an ethic concerned with guiding sexual behavior to have anything to say about disease, other than sexually transmitted diseases. But the ethical principles we have been discussing, taken together, can be the foundation for care and concern for people who have contracted life-threatening diseases. The principles of mutuality and bodily integrity, particularly, obligate one to take care not to expose others or oneself to risk of infection, and to offer care and comfort to those who suffer from affliction.

It is very important that we use this ethic, as well as all others insofar as they are amenable, not as a bludgeon to blame those whose bodies' integrity is already threatened, but as an opportunity to ask, What are the forces that systemically undermine people's capacity to honor the proffered principles? An ethic should point us to the kinds of persons and communities we want to be. In some instances—and we have to be wise to determine when this is the case—we as persons can not live consistently with an ethic because we do not have the power to do so as long as groups within the community constititue power blocks that shape important conditions of our lives. In these instances, the moral accountability belongs to those power blocks that caused the problems to happen, not to the victims of their policies. In this event, moral principles are wrongly used if they blame individual persons who lack the power to change community conditions. It is more appropriate to attempt historical analysis of previously unaccountable political and economic power, in order to identify where moral responsibility rightfully belongs. In this case, what are the forces that systemically undermine people's bodily integrity and their capacity to develop and follow a life plan?

As an illustration, rather than blaming women for lifestyles that may have increased their risk of breast cancer, it is more appropriate to do the necessary research on cancer clusters in the vicinity of nuclear power plants, polluted rivers, and toxic waste sites (where there are also high incidents of birth deformities); if a causal relation between air and water pollution and breast cancer exists, use the ethic to curtail the pollution. Another illustration regards HIV/AIDS. Some scientists have hypothesized that AIDS passed into the human population when humans made military and commercial incursions into geographical areas hitherto undeveloped. If this hypothesis proves to have merit, rather than blame people's HIV/AIDS on their acts (unless they knowingly took risks involving unsafe sexual behavior or drug use, in which case they then share some of the responsibility), better to confront the development projects that make incursions upon tropical forests, thereby bringing people into contact with infectious diseases for which they have not built immunities while at the same time destroying the natural reservoir of therapeutic pharmaceuticals.

Of course, often responsibility is both personal and institutional, as when tobacco companies continue to develop markets for products knowing their health effects on their users, and at the same time people continue to smoke knowing smoking causes lung cancer and exacerbates asthma in nearby nonsmokers. An ethic is not valid if it encourages blame to be given where it is not due; and an ethic proves useful if its principles encourage us to locate all parties to whom responsibility appropriately belongs.

The progressive sexual ethic also provides guidance in relation to health care in general. It gives us as patients the voice to say how our treatments will procede. At the same time, mutuality and the celebration of our embodied selves can help us to honor all stages of growth, as all people are moving toward death, some more aware of death's imminence than others.

The claims of persons with life-threatening diseases to their bodily integrity have economic implications. In order for persons to play a positive role in their own treatment, all people need adequate health care, and this means health care that supports a range of treatment alternatives. Lack of access to health care is one of the most obstinate barriers to economic justice today.

Procreative Choice and Population Concerns

Will the progressive sexual ethic help us to meet the challenges posed by the world's human population growth rate of 95 million people a year, which, according to the U. S. National Academy of Sciences and the Royal Society of London, is the principal cause of the destruction of the world's forests, global warming, and the unparalleled pace of extinction of species?[26]

Concerns about human population growth must be coupled with drastic criticism of the Northern Hemisphere's high rate of resource consumption and dominant models for unsustainable extraction of raw materials, production, development, and economic growth. Yet the human population both North and South is appropriating the earth's biosystems for its own use so quickly that we are losing the capacity to heal the earth. Can the progressive sexual ethic provide guidance in resolving this crisis? Does it help each possible parent consider parenthood with the world's population in mind? Does it help all of us to concern ourselves with, devise, vote for, and support ways to achieve a population level that is sustainable? I believe we have just begun to formulate a procreation ethic that individual persons can use to make personal decisions. The progressive sexual ethic is a good beginning, but we have far to go to achieve helpful specificity to guide us at a public policy level to address population concerns.

Critics of the right to procreative choice in the progressive sexual ethic may claim it promotes having as many children as one wants, regardless of the consequences. But the theologians who derived the ethic believe, and I would state more strongly, that rights are accompanied by duties to use them wisely. We must exercize our rights while taking into consideration our responsibilities toward those who depend on us and the effects our actions will have on those who are less powerful. By claiming women should have rights to procreative choice, we do not mean that any reproductive decision a woman will make will be justifiable, but we do mean that there is no other person or social entity who can be trusted to have the moral insight necessary for making a justifiable decision except the woman whose body and life plan will be affected by that decision.

The right to procreative choice includes the right to access to contraception. As of 1991, approximately 500 million married women worldwide expressed the desire for access to birth control but could not obtain methods suitable to their needs.[27] Lack of access is the result of several factors, including but not limited to lack of medical support structures to provide family planning information, the long distance people must travel to such clinics, and non-health-related restrictions (such as religious proscriptions) on the import, sale, and distribution of contraceptives. Regional surveys indicate that 50 to 60 percent of couples in Latin America, 60 to 80 percent in low-income Asian countries (except China), 75 percent in the Middle East and North Africa, and 90 percent in sub-Saharan Africa do not use any form of modern contraception.[28] Yet the majority of couples in Latin America and Asia, and a growing percentage throughout the Middle East and Africa, wish to space the timing or limit the number of their children.[29] Clearly there is an unmet need for contraception among married couples, and among teenagers and single people as well, worldwide. Availability of contraception would also dramatically lower maternal mortality rates by reducing the number of unsafe illegal abortions.[30]

In order to support the right to a life plan, particularly with respect to contraception, a whole community's resources must be mobilized. This is an excellent example of why life plans are not only individual projects but also require community involvement, even national policy.

Access to a range of contraceptives is clearly needed to support the capacity of people to plan their lives, but we are told by earth-watchers that simply providing birth control technology through family planning programs does not solve the problem of population growth worldwide. Birth control programs alone account for only 15 to 20 percent of overall fertility decline in developing countries, with social and economic factors accounting for the rest.[31] This is not to say that family planning programs are not a crucial component of procreative choice—they are. But they do not by themselves create all the conditions required for their own effectiveness, because high birthrates are associated with poverty. Couples have more children when

- the infant mortality rate is high, so that couples feel they need to have enough children to create a large enough pool so that enough will survive;
- children play an important economic role in bringing resources into the family, and providing retirement security for their parents;
- larger families carry more weight in community affairs;
- there is a "lottery mentality" (with no reliable channels for advancement in sight, parents can always hope that the next child will be the clever one that will get an education and a city job, despite the odds);
- women are socially powerless, get their identities primarily in relationship to their husbands, and receive status primarily in relation to the number of children, particularly sons, they bear;
- women are not powerful enough in relation to their male partners to determine whether they will get pregnant, or how often;
- women do not have access to reproductive health services.[32]

While there is an association between poverty and high fertility, an increase in gross national product (GNP) will not necessarily decrease poverty or fertility. Fertility has declined in some developing countries with little or no industrial development, while some countries have begun to industrialize without an effect on their high rates of fertility. This lack of correlation between development and lower fertility can be attributed in part to the fact that in some industrializing nations the benefits of increased incomes has not been equitably distributed among the population, and to the fact that not all nations have made intentional efforts to use national resources to provide education and health care for the base of the population.[33]

As we have seen, the factors that are important in determining fertility are directly related to conditions for women and families, not to overall development per se. The critical prerequisites to reduced fertility are adequate nutrition, proper sanitation, basic health care, education of women, and equal rights for women.[34] Education is especially important: women tend to apply even a few years of schooling to improving life for their families by providing more nutritious, balanced meals and better home health care and sanitation, while men use education to earn better incomes. Improving home life and health reduces infant and child mortality, making women and men more receptive to the idea of smaller families. Education of women makes them more open to contraception and better able to employ it properly. Finally, when women have sources of status other than children, family sizes decline.[35]

Women's status is thus of central significance to the health of the planet. According to Jodi Jacobson, of the Worldwatch Institute,

> Having done little to remedy the conditions underlying high fertility, governments and international agencies now seek to reduce quickly the rate at which the earth's population is growing. But experience shows that quick fixes—programs aimed more at curtailing birth rates than at improving women's health and productivity—do not work precisely because they do not address fundamental issues like gender bias. . . . The eroding status of low-income women in developing countries is a baseline indicator of human progress. Ignoring this issue is not only morally untenable; it is in the long run self-defeating. Until gender bias is confronted, there can be no sustainable development.[36]

When public funding for health, education, nutrition, and sanitation are distributed throughout the population, and when cultural reform is directed toward the inclusion of women in the social sphere, people have internal motivations for keeping their families small. Policies to spread public resources will require democratic reforms in many cases, particularly where such resources are now being used to fund military weapons expenditures, which are in turn used to coerce people from participating in democratic movements—especially union organizing. A commitment to procreative choice shapes the whole community's use of resources.

Negative rights that prevent coercion from excluding people from participating in democratic processes, plus positive rights to medical care, contraception, and community infrastructures such as sanitation, are both necessary for women to participate in their communities with dignity. The health of the planet and the inclusion of women in determining the conditions of our lives depend on the emerging view of human rights that undergirds the argument for procreative choice in the progressive sexual ethic.[37]

Consistent with the notion that rights are historically defined, the progressive sexual ethic provides the basis for calling all persons to account for discipline in reproductive matters. At this point in the history of the earth, with life-support systems for the whole planet being undermined, a minimal condition for living in community with dignity is community-based, women-designed and -implemented, men-supported, public education programs to solicit voluntary support of an effort to limit our fertility. This effort can not take place instead of social programs guaranteeing basic nutrition, sanitation, education, and equal rights; rather it must accompany them, both in the two-thirds of the world called "underdeveloped" and in the overdeveloped world.

Some people may in good conscience be convinced there is no time for such social and political transformation, and that negative incentives or forms of coercion are the only way to lower fertility rates quickly enough. But at this point persuasion has scarcely been tried in many countries, and there is certainly a role for leadership by religious institutions in desacralizing procreation.[38] I am particularly critical of what I perceive to be the churches' current morality.[39] Church leaders seem to believe that it is right to wait to use proactive fertility-lowering measures until there are so many people that famine or widespread malnutrition is the result; then they consider measures that violate the rights to privacy and bodily integrity (such as requiring women or men to be sterilized, for instance) as the "lesser of evils." Public authorities, including the churches, are way behind in fulfilling their responsibility to ask for voluntary limits on fertility.

We deserve to enjoy nothing that will negate the requirements of dignity for others or imperil the biosphere. The factors that result in lower fertility rates overlap precisely with the requirements for procreative choice. This language of reproductive choice is adaptable enough to take seriously our current historical context—overpopulation of the whole earth—and at the same time support freedom from coercion and access to positive entitlements. We do not have to choose to support only procreative choice or only ecological health; we can support both at the same time by extending basic rights to people who do not have them, by supporting the equality of women, and by sustaining our capacities to be responsible. This is good news. It indicates a social and political strategy for the future, and it confirms the value of the notion of procreative choice we have been exploring. We have the basis for hope that what sustains human dignity is consistent with what sustains the health of all creation.

Patriarchy, Male Identity, and Economic Dislocation

In recent years two Protestant denominations have convened special task forces to provide moral and theological leadership to their churches on human sexuality. Those task force reports that have been consistent with the ethic explored here have been met with extreme resistance and controversy.[40] Considering the force of the objections such studies generated within their denominations, we might ask ourselves why the subject matter of sexual ethics creates such hostility and anger.

Sexual ethics give direction to the social form wherein people seek and express affiliation, intimacy, and for some, the desire for progeny. The progressive sexual ethic challenges the social form of the patriarchal family, which does not honor mutuality, bodily integrity, sex-role fluidity, the possibility of same-sex couples having families, or women's right to a life plan. Because the patriarchal family is threatened by this sexual ethic, many people fear that the family itself is threatened. They do not believe that families without "headship," or male heads of families, can exist or thrive.

Furthermore, this ethic challenges the whole gender structure of masculinity. According to object relations theory, resistance to mutuality and equal regard is psychologically rooted.[41] Because boys have to separate from their first love object, mother, and distance themselves from the female in order to become "masculine," masculinity, the socially constructed way of being male, needs to be proven again and again through rejection of the female and the need for intimacy. Men who work with other men who commit rape and other violence against women have found that the more anxious men are about their own masculine identities, the more angry they become toward gay men for being "womanish."[42] This anger hinges on a deep fear that masculinity is in fact quite fragile, and that rigid roles and economic and political controls are necessary to maintain spheres of male power.[43]

The churches can play an important role in transforming masculine identity away from an identity that is formed by the rejection of females, and toward an identity that is formed by self-love and the love of justice, as modeled by Jesus of Nazareth. But to play this role, church practices and belief systems that hinge on negativity about sex and on the secondary status of women will have to be transformed.

I believe the contemporary conservative obsession with matters pertaining to abortion and sexuality is a substitute for our deep concern about economic security. Ethicist Gerard Fourez finds an analogue in the nineteenth century's focus on sexual ethics: such a focus or obsession, by diverting attention to peripheral elements rather than the central one of a society's structures and practices, makes it possible to conceal problems these structures and practices have created.[44]

Today national boundaries are melting away in the face of treaties supporting the free flow of transnational corporate capital. These economic giants are rarely held accountable for the effects of their investment and disinvestment activities on peoples, land, air, and water—yet the Surgeon General of the United States was fired for acknowledging that masturbation, a way of learning about one's own body and what gives it pleasure, should be discussed in sex education programs. This is clearly an era when major economic dislocation is occuring, while the public, particularly the church-going public, is preoccupied with sexuality. It's high time to learn to do economic ethics.

chapter seven

Economic Ethics

I N THE PRECEDING chapter, we looked at some principles to guide our thinking and acting in the realm of sexuality, acknowledging that we needed a progressive sexual ethic to confront (or at least avoid contributing to) women's secondary economic status. The purpose of this chapter is to consider some principles to guide our thinking and action in the economic sphere itself, in such a way as to result in more justice for women.

Women and Economic Theory

Before we can do economic ethics, we'd better acknowledge that the discipline of economics cannot, without criticism and correction, be our conversation partner. That's because most economists have defined women's work as being outside of the very meaning of "economic" when it does not result in wages or the consumption of cash-paid goods or services. So, for example, women's work in what economists call *reproduction*—cleaning, gathering wood and water, socializing young children, growing food and processing it, cooking, caring for clothing, caring for older children and the elderly and infirm—is not included in calculations of economic activity unless wages are paid for it. Because such "women's work" is invisible to economists, women's claims on public policy makers for their share of the social wealth go unhonored.

New Zealand politician Marilyn Waring has criticized statisticians' exclusion of the value of women's work in the calculation of gross domestic product, even though it is difficult to estimate the value of such work. She asked why it is that women's work in cooking, washing, hauling water, collecting wood, and animal-raising activities cannot be included in calculations of economic activity, while there are arenas of men's unpaid labor that *are* included in gross domestic product, as statisticians find a way to impute value to such activities as sitting in the plaza and talking about neighborhood affairs when men do them (because they are defined as relating to government or security).[1]

Economist John Tiemstra and his colleagues acknowledge the conceptual difficulties of including women's unpaid labor within the realm of "the economic," but say those difficulties have to do with methodological constraints imposed by seemingly neutral scientific ideas in the discipline of economics. The family is often treated in economic theory primarily as the site for consumption, yet most consumption theory is inadequate to account for altruism and other dynamics that characterize decisions about allocating resources within the family.[2] For these and other reasons, characteristics of consumption theory only barely, if at all, fit with the realities of family decision making about labor and resources. These authors also acknowledge that economists ignore a third to a quarter of all economic activity, that which is centered in the family, because economists are only interested in "machismic" (masculine) material. According to Vandana Shiva, the proclivity of the discipline has been to

> disdainfully disregard the economic activity in which women participate most fully and to concentrate on the areas which most directly concern the male ego. This social warping of knowledge has been destructive: it has helped create the powerful myth of female economic parasitism; it has allowed the idea to flourish that only exchange relationships [one good for another, using cash or barter] matter; and it has also led to a whole range of issues which are important to the lives of all of us being summarily dismissed as insignificant.[3]

The choice of what to measure and then include in the realm of the economic is a reflection of what one deems significant enough to develop instruments to measure.

Shiva adds that the focus on exchange relationships in Western economics is rooted in Western science generally, imbued with a Cartesian concept of nature as "environment" or "resource," dualistically separate from humankind. This dualism has given rise to a worldview in which nature is (a) inert and passive, (b) uniform and mechanistic, (c) separable and fragmented within itself, (d) separate from man, and (e) inferior, to be dominated and exploited by man (Shiva uses the term "man" as a gender-specific one). Western science views women as closer to nature than men are, and characterizes them the same way as it characterizes nature; therefore, male control of women's labor is ideologically justified. In this way patriarchal ideology results in the domination of women and also in maldevelopment and ecological crisis.[4]

Who can deny that as a discipline Western economics has been shaped by men—men who do not like to do housework and will get someone else to do it for them, through romance or marriage if possible, for pay if necessary? Male economists are no different from male farmers or male bus drivers in this respect. Men don't do housework because they don't want to. They value other activities more highly. So do many women, but if they do not exert power over household resources in ways that gain them exemption from housework, they do it anyway.

Acknowledging the devaluation of reproductive work in the home and family, and other lapses of economic theory, is an important component of any attempt to redress women's exclusion from economic benefits. Insofar as theory has reinforced the historical devaluation of caretaking and reproduction, for example, women's "energies and power are expended," as Iris Marion Young puts it, "often unnoticed and unacknowledged, usually to benefit men by releasing them for 'more important' and 'more creative' work, enhancing their status or the environment around them, or providing them with sexual or emotional service."[5]

One solution to this problem would involve paying women for housework, though how to finance such payments with any measure of economic justice, that is, without using tax revenues to transfer funds from dual-worker or single-parent households to the relatively advantaged group of housewife-maintaining households, is as yet by no means obvious. Alternatively, we might remove the association between women and housework by splitting all caretaking and reproductive labor, including child care, between husband and wife or partner and partner. This strategy seems promising, though as any woman knows who has tried it, it can have the effect of ending a marriage.[6]

Errors in theory can also result in misbegotten economic policies that hinder women instead of helping them. For example, "development" programs, whether in the industrialized or industrializing worlds, usually deepen rather than challenge gender bias in favor of males, in part because faulty assumptions are implicit in the theory and practice of economic planning. One of these is that within a society economic growth is gender-blind and both men and women will benefit equally from it. A second is that individuals within families have common interests and work toward common goals. A third is that within households, the burdens and benefits of poverty and wealth will be distributed equally regardless of gender. Unfortunately, none of these assumptions is true. Although their faultiness has been documented,[7] simply stating these assumptions may help us to recognize how false they are in our own households, whether in the overdeveloped nations or in the other two-thirds of the world.

Redressing Economic Injustice toward Women

What has our discussion of childbearing and child rearing, sexual harassment, domestic violence, and lesbian identity suggested about how the economic vulnerability of women can be reduced? It appears to me that the most important conclusion is that women should delay marriage (or committed union) and childbirth until their positions in the paid labor force are secure. When both partners are interdependent, healthier family ties can be formed than if one of them is dependent.

Education is central to most women's ability to formulate life plans and pursue them. There is a strong correlation between obtaining higher levels of education and remaining single and childless during young adulthood; for every additional year of education that U.S. women achieve, we postpone our first child by approximately a year.

Education is highly determinative of women's access to the job market, and is thereby key for the ability of women to develop life plans. The knowledge that jobs are available that pay a decent wage helps prevent childbearing from becoming a default income-, status-, or identity-generating strategy. Yet in the job market, job segregation and the wage gap are two phenomena that interfere with women's capacity to earn sufficiently for ourselves, our families, or our futures, and the effects of job segregation and the wage gap are compounded by racism. Affirmative action legislation is still crucial to counteract job segregation. Pay equity realignments of wage scales consistent with the Equal Pay Act passed by Congress in 1963, and the Civil Rights Act of 1964, are needed to address the wage gap.

Because most parents lack paid parental leaves, women will pay the cost of childbearing through lost wages even if they do enter the labor market. Additionally, the biological capacity of women to bear children serves as the rationale for limiting women to "women's jobs" and lower pay than men doing comparable work. Three directions are needed to challenge and reverse this ideology of women's secondary value in the paid labor force. One of these is more social support for a range of child care measures that will assure parents that their children are being well cared for by competent care givers while the parents are working. Another is parental support policies that will provide some income to new mothers and fathers who take leave, and social encouragement of fathers to be as responsible for the care of children as women are currently held to be. And, finally, employers should be as innovative in structuring work as they are in product development, so that shorter work weeks, flex-time, and job sharing opportunities proliferate.

To prevent sexual harassment, which hinders women's participation in the paid labor force, the desegregation of all job categories is again important. Where there is gender integration on the job, blatant experiences of sexual pressure diminish and ambiguous incidents can be handled informally. When sexual harassment does occur, it should be treated as the law defines it, as a form of sex discrimination, and should be punished by a law enforcement agency if the employer will not do so. Since sexual harassment has such powerful effects on people's economic stability, it should be treated as a threat to normal freedom of movement and security, and not as a form of free speech to be protected.

To prevent domestic violence, all the above efforts are needed. In addition, there is a place for two further efforts. The first is criminalization of spouse abuse, whether the abused partner wishes to make a complaint or not. Criminalization is a way of countering the cultural expectation that people have a right to use violence in intimate relationships. This program is primarily dependent upon changes in implementation of the law. The second effort needed is public funding for emergency shelters for women and children, and then for second-stage and transitional housing for those women and children as they develop their long-term strategies for living free from abuse. Emergency, second-stage, and transitional housing will require tax supports. While some users may be able to pay rent, sheltering does not generate income sufficient to meet the cost, and hence some stable public funding will be required. Such public funding could be offset in part by wages attached from violent perpetrators, who *owe* their ex-partners and children compensation for their irresponsible behavior but will likely not give it to them voluntarily.

Lesbian women do not escape the liabilities associated with childbirth and child rearing, sexual harassment, and domestic violence. A lesbian woman can have children from a prior marriage, with the cooperation of a sperm donor, or through adoption. She may experience the same sexual harassment as all women do, even if her coworkers know she is not heterosexual. She can also experience domestic violence from her woman partner.

Furthermore, lesbian women are vulnerable to homophobia, which affects lesbian women's economic stability as much as it affects gay men's. The measures needed to protect lesbian women as lesbians are predominantly legal remedies: judicial reforms to guarantee freedom from antigay discrimination in family conflicts, child custody, job hiring and firing, and private consensual sex among adults. These measures will give lesbian and gay people the same protections that heterosexual people now enjoy.

Is it possible to imagine a woman-friendly economy—that is, one that does not exact more from women than from men? If we could imagine it, would we want such an economy? That is the task of economic ethics, and of the rest of this book.

A Religious Inheritance for Economic Ethics

In order to do economic ethics, we first have to understand that economics is an appropriate arena for ethical reflection. Economics is not simply a science; the sole task for economists is not simply to understand ever more clearly how various factors create or fail to create goods and services. An economy is a pattern of relations that organize a society's activities of production, distribution, and consumption. They include laws that protect relationships, institutions, and values that honor some behaviors over others and some "goods" over others. An economic system is a way of managing a household, whether that household represents an individual, family, city, nation, or the Earth itself. The way we manage our household(s) both reflects and shapes our character. That is why economics is a thoroughly moral matter. "Economic choices of the members and institutions of a society reflect what a society is and influence what it is becoming."[8]

We don't come to the effort to imagine a woman-friendly economy empty-handed. We have a legacy of religious principles for economic justice and some of them are very pertinent to redressing women's economic vulnerability. I'll review them here, indicating where I commend the teachings as well as where I challenge them. Although these teachings are religious in their formulations, I do not offer them for consideration because of their religious authority alone. Scriptures, traditions, and the teaching authority of religious groups are sometimes helpful and sometimes terribly harmful. The test of their validity is their capacity to help us to be the best people we can be in the best communities we can nurture into being. Arguably, the reason a scripture is Scripture is that it has helped past communities to answer these questions. But we cannot grant the scriptures of any tradition or any other religious authority unqualified or uncritical acceptance. For example, sections of the Bible reflect a view of women and children as property rather than as full human beings. The Bible also justifies religious and ethnic aggression, a view that few people now accept.

The motivations undergirding the religious social teachings I am reviewing here are also open to challenge. Motivations do not constitute the whole moral quality of teachings, since people can intend evil while producing good effects; however, motivations are certainly morally relevant, and suspect motives may qualify compelling messages.

While I focus primarily on Roman Catholic social teachings regarding what constitutes economic justice, the teachings of many if not most of the Protestant denominations are quite consistent with respect to these matters. Protestants and Catholics have serious disagreements about other issues, such as the permissability of ordaining women and gay men, the possible justification of abortion, and the nature of population concerns. But there is by and large a shared perspective among these various denominations regarding economic justice. I want to extend this shared perspective and apply it to stakeholders whose voices have not been adequately heard in these traditions—to include the voices of women, some with children.

I believe these social teachings have potential in this regard because together they constitute a significant confrontation with the dominant liberal capitalist economic culture that lets the marketplace determine accessibility to the goods and services necessary for human dignity. Consistent with my view that economics is thoroughly political and moral in character, I believe we cannot leave to "impersonal market forces" the provision of those securities we deem to be most basic to human dignity, because "the market" has been engendered male. We may be able to use market mechanisms for provision of such basic securities, but only after the political process has rebalanced the value of women's work, whether paid or unpaid.

What are these teachings? They are most sharply articulated in a body of statements whose origin is usually identified as Pope Leo XIII's encyclical *Rerum Novarum* (On the Condition of Workers). That document was written in 1891, primarily to preserve the "one true faith" at a time when working-class Catholics were disaffiliating from the church and turning to socialist labor politics. Although Leo and other popes have been accused of wanting to preserve an "organic" society in which the church would remain dominant, the Catholic church was in fact less quickly seduced into an uncritical perspective on free-market liberal capitalism than Protestantism was. From the repository of potentially critical principles I'll select some key examples to illustrate the contributions of Roman Catholic social teachings to a critical evaluation of free-market absolutism.

The accountability of capital to justice in productive relations
Because of the power differential between employers and workers, contracts between employers and employees are not freely negotiated. Thus contracts must be subject to moral constraints in addition to freedom, particularly to the constraints of justice. Capitalists should provide workers a just wage, one that is sufficient for family needs and allows the accumulation of some property by the workers. And capitalists should not provide working conditions that are degrading or threaten the health of workers. Private property cannot be amassed or used in ways that are contrary to distributive justice and the dignity of all persons.

The accountability of private property to the common good
Private property is necessary for people's capacity to exercise autonomy in their lives, substantiating and giving a base to their freedom to be responsible for themselves and their families. However, the right to private property is not an absolute right, for it is accountable to the common good. In the language of *Rerum Novarum*,

> No one is commanded to distribute to others that which is required for [one's] own necessities and those of [one's] household; nor even to give away what is reasonably required to keep up becomingly [one's] condition in life; for no one ought to live unbecomingly. But when necessity has been supplied, and one's position fairly considered, it is a duty to give to the indigent out of that which is left over.[9]

The just entitlement of the poor to necessities from the luxury of the nonpoor is therefore a corollary to this principle.

The duty of government to protect the poor
Since it is through the labor of the poor that material well-being

is constructed, and since the poor are most vulnerable to exploitation and least able to protect themselves, the duty of justice requires governments to protect the interest of the poor. Governments fulfill this obligation when the poor are housed, clothed, and enabled to support life. If there is a conflict between the rights of the poor and the rights of others, it is the duty of the public authority to give special consideration to the poor.

The obligation to make payment on the social mortgage

The social mortgage is the debt all must pay back to a society in recognition that one inherits wealth in the form of goods or knowledge or technology from those who have gone before or who walk with us now. The social mortgage is a principle of return.[10] It acknowledges, like composting does, that the foundations of (social) life must be replenished if they are to continue to nourish us. We can pay our share of the social mortgage in various ways—for example, by providing low- or no-interest loans for low-income housing out of a portion of one's holdings, contributing fully one's share of taxes used to support social programs, or giving a percentage of one's income directly to services for the poor and otherwise vulnerable.

The principle of subsidiarity

The state and the law must protect communities, families, and individuals. Social problems must be dealt with at the lowest possible level of social and political organization at which they can be addressed successfully—in the family, the neighborhood, a parish, a school system, a business—which protects the autonomy of small- and intermediate-sized social groupings. Yet we must involve ever higher levels of social and political organization until issues can be addressed appropriately—the city, the state, the federal government, or the international world order.[11]

Participation as an aspect of economic justice

In the 1986 pastoral letter entitled *Economic Justice for All*, the U.S. Conference of Catholic Bishops viewed participation in the economy to be exercised primarily through employment and widespread ownership of property. The principle of participation is antithetical to paternalism, and is consistent with the principle of subsidiarity.[12]

A Legacy to Overcome

In addition to the useful principles above, Christian social teachings about economics also contain some elements that make the struggle for economic justice for women very difficult to wage within the churches. One principle is particularly ignoble: the principle that inequality is just. The agenda of Pope Leo XIII in *Rerum Novarum* was to renounce socialism, so the encyclical assumes capitalism, though capitalism with a human face. The pope denounced socialism in part because of its challenge to religious authority; he was reacting to socialist activists who exposed class conflict and encouraged working people to develop a loyalty to their own class rather than to their employers or their employers' church. In addition, he was reacting to a mistaken notion that a socialist program would collectivize all property, and to the expressed commitment of socialist movements to social equality for all.

> Humanity must remain as it is. It is impossible to reduce human society to a level. The Socialists may do their utmost, but all striving against nature is vain. There naturally exist among mankind innumerable differences of the most important kind. People differ in capability, in diligence, in health, and in strength; and thus inequality in fortune is a necessary result of inequality in condition. Such inequality is far from being disadvantageous either to individuals or to the community. Social and public life can go on only by the help of various kinds of capacity and the playing of many parts, and each man, as a rule, chooses the part which peculiarly suits his case.[13]

One wonders if the special duty of government to consider the interests of the poor is an easier principle to promote than one of removing the structural conditions allowing the rich to emerge as a class in the first place while a great many other people become poor.[14]

The principle that inequality is just also appears in Protestant writings.[15] From the time of the early church it has been claimed that the poor are entitled to goods to satisfy their necessities, even if they must take them from the rich.[16] Yet this claim has always rested on the assumption of a class society in some form, where there would always be rich and poor. The occasional outbreaks of economic and political egalitarianism in the Protestant tradition, for instance among the sixteenth-century Anabaptists, are regarded as heretical by most Catholics and as excessive by Lutheran and Calvinist Protestants.[17]

Does present-day Christianity tacitly support economic inequality? Recent declarations do affirm the equality of women and men in every aspect of our common life,[18] and support economic equity and fairness.[19] But readers beware! Fairness is another word for justice, and some people believe it is quite just for investors to be rewarded for risk taking while workers lose wages, benefits, and even their jobs to allow the corporation to yield a higher rate of return for shareholders. Many people believe fairness to be quite consistent with vastly unequal rewards from the economic system.

Equity, on the other hand, is a term connoting compromise. If there is seemingly irresolvable conflict over approaches to justice, such as when one party emphasizes satisfaction of basic needs while another believes in differential rewards depending upon different amounts of production and a third party believes only equal rewards are just, equity is the mark of a resolution of the conflict so that the validity of conflicting views is acknowledged. The capacity to approach equity is very important, and we will always be seeking it. But equity, though it sounds similar, is in no way the same as equality. Equality, as you can see, may be in conflict with both needs and works as measures of justice. Equity may call for equality, but then again it very well may not.

The Implications of Women's Experience

How would the principles of economic justice change if we used as our point of departure not the authority of church or tradition, but rather the experience of women who are vulnerable economically?

Some would not change at all. The accountability of capital to justice in productive relations, for instance, is as relevant and challenging to the status quo now as it was in 1891. Contracts between employers and employees must still be subject to the constraints of justice. And employers still often fail to meet this requirement. For example, some companies still work to undermine unions and thus remove the major mechanism working people have had to ensure they enter bargaining situations with some power. New forms of injustice have also arisen. For instance, employers have been hiring women and men out of separate labor markets, and the wage level for a particular job title in a particular establishment may be set after the employer decides whether those jobs will be filled by women or men. A particular job pays substantially more in a firm that hires primarily men to fill it than the same job in a comparable firm that hires primarily women for that position.[20] Discrimination prevents women from being able to "freely negotiate" their wages.

The duty of the government to protect the poor is another unchanging principle. It has an immediate relevance to our contemporary context, where low- and moderate-income housing is in increasingly short supply and the homeless, including abused women and their children, are those least able to compete for it in the market. Instead of decreasing governmental involvement in housing, as the Reagan and Bush administrations did, there should be a renewed commitment to governmental support for low- and moderate-income housing stock.

Some of these principles take on new meaning or specificity when viewed in light of women's economic vulnerability. For instance, the principle of subsidiarity has new meaning in relationship to the provision of high-quality child care. High-quality child care requires care giver stability, yet child center staff positions are among the highest in turnover. Care giver stability requires good working conditions and respectable salaries, yet care givers are among the lowest paid of all workers. High-quality child care requires a low child-to-care-giver ratio and small group size. It requires safe play structures and toys, plus rooms and furnishings that absorb noise and create a variety of environments. In other words, high-quality child care is expensive. Child care cannot be left to market forces, as advocated by those who value consumer freedom and dislike government involvement; the market left to itself will always attempt to decrease the cost per child; hence what's good for the market is bad for the child. Markets may be used, created, and regulated to good advantage in child care economics, but a social commitment to the well-being of children must first be made.[21]

The principle of subsidiarity stipulates that social problems must be dealt with at the lowest possible level of society where they can be addressed successfully. The solution to the child care problem must occur on a combination of levels—family, neighborhood, city, county, state, and nation. We have the benefit of the example of successful efforts in other industrialized countries, who finance good quality child-care by combining national, state, and local subsidies with parent fees. A system wherein individuals choose in an impersonal market may have satisfactory results for the wealthy, but to provide good care for all our children, policy guaranteeing social support is required.

A second example of the way traditional principles can be applied to contemporary situations is this: the accountability of private property to the common good means, among other things, the accountability of capital to community stability. This principle is antithetical to economic policies promoting the mobility of capital over the interests of the labor force. If companies want our markets, then we have something to bargain with, and I believe we should be debating the most effective accountability structures rather than negotiating free trade agreements.[22] Until we are serious about holding capital accountable for its effects on community stability, we will have no hope for enduring communities. Without stable industries, our communities are deprived of the tax bases they need to undergird social programs and we have high unemployment, particularly among male workers who traditionally entered the labor force through manufacturing. When those men go into the underground economy as an alternative to the low-wage service sector, they are less likely to marry or to support their offspring.

Local community stability is a necessary way for entrepreneurs and others to pay their share of the social mortgage. Any production of wealth occurs in a place where people live, where there is a geography and an ecology. When business is not held accountable for its effects on particular communities—or when people are forced to become itinerant or temporary workers, unable to develop or sustain roots—then there is little social authority to collect on the social mortgage and little motivation for businesses to pay it. In addition, the social mortgage is a principle of return not only to people but also to other species. We are now looking for appropriate methods of guaranteeing that people don't take from other species more than can be paid back; already we are destroying species' habitats and thus these species themselves.

Local community stability is, consequently, one objective that should serve as a major criterion for evaluating economic policies. Women have a stake in local community stability, particularly when these communities exercise the self-rule prescribed by the principle of subsidiarity. In such communities, not only is there a capacity to plan for social programs such as child care and emergency and second-stage shelters, but in social situations characterized by local control women are frequently leaders along with men. When power is hierarchialized, women generally seem to lose leadership positions.

In fact, in order to increase women's participation at all levels of the economy, I believe we will need to orient policy toward decentralization (not deregulation) as well as toward community stability. Decentralization is the economic basis for community self-rule, whereby communities emphasize use of raw materials from the regions in which they are located. While the exact size of such communities is an open question, and while there is no virtue in isolationism, the use of regional raw materials makes possible local control of ownership patterns, and allows the exclusion of large national or international corporations, should the localities legislate it. I recommend a step-by-step approach to decentralization, beginning with decentralization of energy, which provides the foundation for all the other sectors of the economy.

The formulation of a policy for decentralization of energy as a case study and a place to begin can benefit from a sector approach to economics, one which analyzes a particular area of the economy (e.g., housing, agriculture, health care) that is an essential part of the structure that supports a whole population. Although sector analysis relating to women and the economy has been limited, I hope that more political economists will look to this technique in the future.[23] Otherwise we will be limited in our visioning to the question of whether women should be oriented toward the paid labor force or not, the paid labor force being defined by jobs that men design, advertise for, fill, and pay for.

Currently, most energy systems in the United States are highly capital intensive investments. They involve central power stations, oil refineries, or nuclear reactors, which require years and years of lead time to plan and finance and then are so expensive that there is a strong temptation to skimp on shut-down time for routine maintenance and repairs because of the financial consequences. Because they are centralized, they make whole regions vulnerable to loss of power service in the event of severe weather, natural disaster, or sabotage. They are controlled by a central technical elite, associated with remote and unaccountable institutions; users cannot understand, repair, or modify the energy sources on which they depend.[24]

A less brittle and more resilient energy system would use more dispersed, diverse, local, and redundant modules. It might even be cheaper; while we expect the big power plants to achieve economies of scale, large-scale energy technologies are not inherently cheaper, and may be costlier, than those scaled to match their end uses, most of which are relatively small and dispersed.[25] Small-scale energy technologies include cogeneration plants in factories, wind machines for domestic and institutional use, and passive solar energy. They have the advantage of using energy sources that are renewable and thus consistent with the principle of sustainability.

In their book *Brittle Power*, Amory Lovins and L. Hunter Lovins argue persuasively for these technologies:

> A simple example illustrates how much renewable sources can simplify the energy system and get rid of its most vulnerable parts. One way (currently the most popular) to obtain light when one flicks the switch is to pay people hundreds of miles away to do the dirty, dangerous job of digging coal out of the ground and shipping it by rail or barge to a power plant somewhere else. There the coal is burned, releasing the energy stored in it by sunlight which

fell on a primeval swamp millions of years ago. The flames make high-pressure steam which spins a huge turbine which runs a generator. Giant transformers step up the voltage for transmission over long aerial lines to one's part of the country, where the voltage is again stepped down through several stages of subtransmission and distribution, and eventually brought through a wire into one's home. . . . But another alternative is to install on one's roof a device which converts today's sunlight directly into electricity, with no fuel, moving parts, noise, smell, or attention.[26]

Energy systems need to be chosen that will work best in the context of each region's different weather patterns. If an area is cloudy, making photovoltaic cells impractical, it is probably good for wind power; if dry, it will be good for solar cells. Intermittance in a given source of renewable energy can be planned for, just as hydroelectric projects plan for variation in water flow. And integration of two or more renewable energy systems multiplies the ways to reduce total energy costs.

Decentralized energy systems are also good for national security. Centralized energy sources are vulnerable to sabotage; the likelihood of accidents in nuclear power plants threatens the health of whole communities; and reliance on foreign supplies of petroleum encourages U.S. involvement in war.

Nuclear power is the opposite of sustainable, decentralized energy. No one knows how to dispose of nuclear waste safely, yet nuclear power plants continue to generate it. And because the nuclear industry cannot safely dispose of its wastes, related costs are passed on to the public even though they are not included in the electric rates; the public is presented with a false energy statement, and hence people think nuclear power is cheap.[27] In time the truth will out about the extent to which nuclear contamination threatens public health, about the fact that individuals pay a portion of these hidden energy costs in their medical bills. When the nation gets beyond denial and begins to clean up the results of ineffective nuclear waste disposal in the environment, we will pay again through taxes.

By decreasing the levels at which local governments, businesses, and homes have to "import" their energy, we strengthen local governments' revenue bases, the business climate, and the capacity to generate sustainable jobs. The payments for energy stay in the local area, where women can (but not necessarily will) have more say in how resources may be used. Localism has risks as well as rewards: it can be marked by ethnic group exclusivism and patriarchal culture, against which we should be wary. Yet the alternative is riskier; energy systems are so crucial to the possibility of community stability that centralized, highly capitalized energy virtually ensures a threat to local economic stability. With decentralized energy there is the material basis for economic as well as political democracy.[28] Decentralization is necessary, though not sufficient, to support participation of women in the community's economic policy making.

The principle of sustainability has appeared in Catholic and Protestant religious economic ethics only recently, but I find it another way of specifying what the accountability of power and private property to the common good requires today. Sustainability involves living within the regenerative capacities of the earth. It is a principle of return, like payment on the social mortgage. Work and all other contributions women traditionally make to society are not recognized or valued commensurate with men's contributions, yet the reproduction of life and its nurturance is absolutely necessary and productive for the economy and community well-being. Sustainability as a principle requires a new way of calculating consequences and growth, beyond GNP to what economist Herman Daly and ethicist John Cobb, Jr., call the Index of Sustainable Welfare.[29] This principle connects ecological integrity to economic justice for women.

Challenging Inequality

When we evaluate the legacy of religious principles regarding economic justice in light of the failure of the economy to serve women and children, we find that those discussed so far in this chapter remain valid, though what it means to implement them is contingent on the demands of our era. But reflection on women's experience in the economy leads us to *challenge* one principle in the tradition: the principle of inequality. Principles for economic justice should incorporate the principle of equality if the goal is truly the *common* good rather than the good of men. Gender equality would redress each of the problem areas discussed earlier in the following ways:

Reflecting on the effects of childbearing, it is not fair to treat women who have young children equally—that is, the same as—women and men who do not, because there are morally relevant differences in their situations. And yet it is also not fair to treat all women as though we are mothers of young children, especially since protective social policies nearly always result in inequality because they function as disincentives for employers to hire women. So justice for all women requires parental policies that apply to both fathers and mothers of young children. We need family policies that give economic stability to women who are single parents and that at the same time encourage fathers to be parents. This is a move toward *gender equality*, one which depends on recognizing the need for special support, that is, a difference in treatment, for parents and others with significant dependent care responsibilities.

Reflecting on the causes and effects of domestic violence, it is very clear to me that the reason our culture has not mobilized more effectively to punish violent men and to protect vulnerable women is that we are still subject to the cultural memory of a time when women were property. We do not fully believe women are the moral equals of men. We believe, in some corner of our collective psyche, that men know better than women what is good for them, and thus that men have the right to control women. The fractures caused by domestic violence can only be healed in relationships marked by equality.

Reflecting on sexual harassment, we need to learn from the fact that it occurs less in sexually desegregated work groups than in other settings. When women make up at least one-third of the group, sexual harassment either does not occur or can be neutralized before it becomes significant to any person targeted. In order to promote this kind of environment, the labor force must be desegregated so that the supervisor, as well as the supervisee, is as likely to be a woman as a man. Equality once again is an economic factor, a concrete criterion of relations that will assure women justice.

Reflecting on the effects of lesbian identity, we see that for morally irrelevant reasons, lesbians and gay men are economically vulnerable. Economic justice demands that they not face discrimination relating to their sexuality, and that their work be evaluated on equal terms with that of heterosexuals.

The egalitarianism I affirm here is not the simple or mechanical equality that requires totalitarianism to sustain it, nor is it the so-called equality of opportunity that coexists (though uncomfortably) with extreme racial and economic inequality. The economic program of the Hebrew Scriptures, reaffirmed in Jesus' ministry as recorded particularly in the gospel of Luke, reflects a commitment to a community life in which the burdens as well as the benefits of life together fall similarly on all. One economist calls this a basic commitment to "limited inequality," and this is a qualifier I will accept.[30] But that qualification only makes sense in the context of a primary vision of social and therefore economic equality.

Because of individual quirks, the luck of the draw, historical factors beyond anyone's control, individuals' freely chosen priorities, and perhaps even their sins, total economic equality cannot be sustained for even the lifespan of one generation. In recognition of this, scriptures in Leviticus and Deuteronomy require a periodical "mid-course correction"—a jubilee, every fifty years—to wipe the slate clean of all debts. The jubilee was a mechanism to prevent the establishment of rigid social classes, to mitigate against the tendency toward the consolidation of landholding in the hands of the few and thereby to maintain a landed peasantry that could provide for themselves, their families, and their futures with sufficiency, though certainly not luxury.

Leviticus 26 is very clear that the economic practice of preventing extremes of both wealth and poverty is a religious duty, part of the covenant with Yahweh: one cannot be faithful to Yahweh and ignore the economic program, and if the people do ignore it, warfare will come to the land, the earth will cease to be fertile, and families will be torn asunder; if people maintain the practice of the jubilee, there will be political and social harmony, the vineyards and croplands will be productive, and families will be able to provide for themselves. One gets the picture that peace and ecological and economic harmony require that inequality be limited.

Jesus of Nazareth challenged some provisions of the Mosaic code in which the jubilee appears, those that constituted a purity code that stigmatized innocent people, including women and ethnic groups that were not Jews, but Jesus affirmed the jubilee itself, because it reversed the hierarchical social order and made possible a society of mutual accountability and equal regard. So people for whom the Hebrew Bible and the New Testament are authorities should be aware that there are economic values that have been given priority in their traditions, and that these values are rooted in a vision of social and economic equality that is qualified by the recognition that people will have to witness and then repeatedly challenge uneven distribution. (That Pope Leo XIII was not informed by this vision of economic value simply confirms the power of the ethical criteria through which one chooses to approach all Scripture. It was not a value for the church of his time, though it was for the socialist movement.)

Reciprocity in the Workplace

Judaism and Christianity are not the only resources for those seeking to model economic equality. Political philosophers such as Carol Gould and Michael Walzer are trying to help us "remember" a commitment to democracy in the economic realm to accompany democracy in the political realm.[31] Until we believe economic democracy is right and valuable enough to struggle for, we will not experience anything near egalitarianism in the political realm, because money can buy power.[32] Thus economic equality involves a committment to economic reciprocity.

Reciprocity is a way of describing mutuality in economic relations. Whereas mutuality as a norm in sexual ethics means primarily equal regard, reciprocity means mutual exchange. It requires structures of fair distribution that flow from people's interdependence in production and reproduction.

Reciprocity is the opposite of exploitation. Using the example of the workplace, exploitation is a relationship in which the owner benefits at the expense of labor because the owner controls the conditions of labor and the activity of the workers and does not give equivalent return for their labor to the workers.[33] Reciprocity, on the other hand, amounts to a requirement of workers' self-management or worker control. Such worker control is suggested as an option in the U.S. Catholic bishops' pastoral letter referred to before, as a way of honoring the principle of participation.[34] Here I suggest it should be a major way to organize production.

When workers elect their own management councils to produce policy in partnership with the professional management team, greater numbers of workers become involved in problem solving and innovation, decreasing the need for the layer of the work force known as supervisors.[35] When workers supervise themselves and each other, productivity is often very high because the workers are producing, whether of goods or of services, in order to create a product they are proud of, to support themselves and their families, and to insure ongoing stability for their own workplace. Essentially, they are supporting themselves and their communities rather than an elite group of management or a class of capitalists whose highest priority is to turn a profit for themselves and their stockholders. Of course, worker involvement does not preclude low salaries, but it generally precludes a vast gap between the lowest salary and the highest.

Theoretically, if workers don't have to support their supervisors they can work fewer hours, and a shorter work week becomes possible. Particularly when parents can spell each other for child care (whether they are married to each other or not), a work week of thirty hours can best serve to decrease the contradiction between work and nurturance that so many parents experience today. Worker self-management as one index of reciprocity has an immediate connection to freeing up time for the "reproductive" sphere of our lives.

In addition, reciprocity is one of the principles underlying comparable pay for comparable work—a policy measure to address the wage gap. Women are paid less for their work, not because it is less productive, less skilled, or less responsible, but solely because it's work women do. Comparable pay is another way of specifying what reciprocity in the economic arena might mean.

Toward a Woman-Friendly Economy

In sum, when we start our moral reflection with a commitment to the dignity and well-being of women who are economically vulnerable, some new specificity and moral insight emerges about what economic justice for all people requires:

1. The principle of *subsidiarity* requires moving child care policy from the private realm and the marketplace to the social realm.
2. Enforcing *accountability of capital to community stability* is a contemporary way of honoring the accountability of power and private property to the common good.
3. *Community stability* involves self-rule and suggests decentralization of major aspects of the economy, beginning with energy production.
4. *Sustainability* is another measure of accountability to the common good, and involves living in a manner that the earth can support, and that promotes the well-being of future generations. Sustainability trumps economic growth as an indicator of economic well-being.
5. *Equality*—gender, racial, and social equality—becomes the most important facet of economic justice.
6. *Reciprocity* challenges all forms of exploitation. It suggests worker control as the major mode of organizing production. It also requires comparable pay for comparable work and implies limits on the time required for productivity outside the home.

There is a very important connection between sexuality and economics in the "lived-world experience" of every woman and every man. Economic justice requires providing women direct access to the economy in our own right, having our contributions valued in both the productive and reproductive spheres. Only when women achieve economic justice will sexual justice be possible. As Beverly Harrison says,

> Economic justice as access to and genuine participation in the production, distribution, and determination of the use of a society's wealth is also a condition of sexual freedom. All distortions of power in society reveal themselves in the inequity of power dynamics in interpersonal life.[36]

I have tried to imagine how to remove the distortions of power that result in women's economic vulnerability, distortions due to the definition of women as sexual persons by a male-dominated social tradition. The economic principles I've put forth are proposed both as standards for evaluating and criticizing the current economic order and as pointers to a future alternative economic system. If we can nourish the political will to reorganize the economy to serve these principles, rather than allowing freedom without accountability and using the market as the sole measure of value, I believe a just and equal commonwealth could emerge, one where women's sexual self-determination would have a material basis.

notes

1. INTRODUCTION

1. See Chaim Perelman, *The Idea of Justice and the Problem of Argument* (London: Routledge & Kegan Paul, 1963), 1–60.

2. Iris Marion Young, *Justice and the Politics of Difference* (Princeton, N. J.: Princeton University Press, 1990), 37.

3. See Elizabeth Achtemeier, "Righteousness in the OT," *Interpreter's Dictionary of the Bible* (Nashville: Abingdon Press, 1962), vol. 4, 80–83; and John R. Donahue, "Biblical Perspectives on Justice," in *The Faith That Does Justice,* ed. John C. Haughey (New York: Paulist Press, 1977), 68–112. Donahue traces shifts in this idea of justice in the intertestamental period and the New Testament, so the account I present here best characterizes the Hebrew Scriptures. Nevertheless, Jesus and Paul are rooted in this notion of justice, Donahue claims, which is particularly exemplified by their expectation of the Kingdom, or reign of God, and the characteristics of the "just man" who lives by faith. Donahue does not explore the continuities between justice as an economic principle and the definition of *koinonia,* as I do later in this chapter.

4. Beverly Wildung Harrison, "The Dream of a Common Language: Towards a Normative Theory of Justice in Christian Ethics," in *The Annual of the Society of Christian Ethics,* ed. Larry L. Rasmussen (Waterloo, Ontario: Council on Study of Religion, Wilfrid Laurier University, 1983), 1–25.

5. Margaret Farley, *Personal Commitments: Beginning, Keeping, Changing* (San Francisco: Harper, 1986), 82–83.

6. In addition to Beverly Harrison and Margaret Farley, many other women have explored the possibilities of using justice to ground their social ethics. For a discussion of some of these recent efforts, see Carol S. Robb, "Women's Contribution to the Meaning of Justice," *Pacific Theological Review* 21, no. 1 (Fall 1987): 38–47; and also Karen Lebacqz, *Justice in an Unjust World: Foundations for a Christian Approach to Justice* (Minneapolis: Augsburg, 1987).

7. Christopher J. H. Wright proposes that the biblical redemption laws had a different function than the jubilee provisions. The main aim of redemption was to preserve the land of the "kin group"; a relative of the impoverished Israelite could redeem property sold to pay a debt, but was not necessarily required to

return the property to the indebted one. The indebted one could certainly re-cover the property if he later had the means, but even if he did not, the jubilee mandated the return of the sold property to the individual household. The re-demption laws kept the property in the kinship group; the jubilee restored it to the household (see Wright, *God's People in God's Land: Family, Land, and Property in the Old Testament* [Grand Rapids: Eerdmans; Exeter, England: Paternoster, 1990], 120–21).

8. I have leaned heavily on three sources for this discussion: Marvin Chaney, "Debt Easement and Debt Remission in the Bible," written for the Presbyte-rian Church (USA) Advisory Committee on Social Witness Policy's Task Force on "Sustainable Development, Reformed Faith, and U.S. International Economic Policy" (1993–94); Jeffrey A. Fager, *Land Tenure and the Biblical Jubilee: Uncovering Hebrew Ethics through the Sociology of Knowledge*, from the *Journal for the Study of the Old Testament* supplement series 155 (Sheffield, England: Sheffield Academic Press, 1993); and Wright, *God's People in God's Land*.

9. I appreciate Marvin Chaney's concern that contemporary readers of the Bible both identify the economic practices contained therein and also refrain from simplistically characterizing that economic system.

10. Chaney, "Debt Easement and Debt Remission," 3.

11. Wright, *God's People in God's Land*, 177.

12. The writers of these texts were using the tradition emerging from village sub-sistence agriculture, but the writers themselves were members of elites affili-ated with one or another political and social formation in Palestine before or after the exile to Babylonia. Why did traditions such as those prohibiting in-terest on survival loans to the poor and the granting of other easements sur-vive the writing and editing of texts by one or another elite? Marvin Chaney argues that the timing of the proclamation of debt easements and releases sug-gests they enabled kings to weaken potential rivals who were wealthy and powerful, to ameliorate economic abuses severe enough to threaten the via-bility of the state, and to project a public image as just statesmen. So while the traditions were rooted in a society that valued limits to inequality, they were used selectively by ruling elites and in that way survived (see Chaney's "Debt Easement in Israelite History and Tradition," in *The Bible and Politics of Exegesis*, ed. David Jobling, Peggy L. Day, and Gerald T. Sheppard [Cleve-land: Pilgrim, 1991], 127–39).

13. Wright, *God's People in God's Land*, 178.

14. See Elisabeth Schüssler Fiorenza, *In Memory of Her: A Feminist Theological Reconstruction of Christian Origins* (New York: Crossroad, 1983); for sum-mary passages see pp. 141, 149, 199, and 216.

15. For this treatment of Jesus' perspectives on the family, sexuality, and children, I use L. William Countryman, *Dirt, Greed, and Sex: Sexual Ethics in the New Testament and Their Implications for Today* (Philadelphia: Fortress, 1988).

16. Elisabeth Schüssler Fiorenza's argument is that "to reconstruct the Jesus movement as a Jewish movement within its dominant patriarchal cultural and religious structures is to delineate the feminist impulse within Judaism" (see *In Memory of Her*, 106–10).

17. Ibid., 148.

18. My colleague and Hebrew Scriptures scholar Marvin Chaney tells me the word used to refer to biblical people up to the Babylonian exile is *Israelite*. After the exile the term *Jewish* is used. *Palestine* is the geographical region and is a name without distinction to period.

19. Countryman, *Dirt, Greed, and Sex*, 168–89; Schüssler Fiorenza, *In Memory of Her*, 146–47.

20. Wright, *God's People in God's Land*, 110–14.

21. Schüssler Fiorenza, *In Memory of Her*, 199.

22. Ibid., 210.

23. Ibid., 218.

24. Ibid., 265.

25. Antoinette Clark Wire, *The Corinthian Women Prophets: A Reconstruction through Paul's Rhetoric* (Minneapolis: Fortress, 1990).

26. Schüssler Fiorenza, *In Memory of Her*, 199.

27. This is the way Wright justifies this claim: in the *koinonia*, the new community shares everything in common (Acts 2:42,44) and ensures that nobody is in need (Acts 4:34); believers are urged to share hospitality with the saints, and the rich are commanded to be generous (1 Timothy 6:18), as are all Christians (Hebrews 13:16); and Paul commended the Corinthians for their eagerness to share in the financial *koinonia* collection as proof of their obedience to the Gospel (see *God's People in God's Land*, 112).

28. Ibid., 113–14.

29. John Reumann, "Koinonia in Scripture: Survey of Biblical Texts," Document No. 5 for the World Council of Churches, Fifth World Conference on Faith and Order, Santiago de Compostello, Spain, 3–14 August 1993, 5.

30. Ibid., 4, 9.

31. Ibid., 10.

32. Schüssler Fiorenza, *In Memory of Her*, 245–79.

33. Ibid., 316–19.

34. Ibid., 35.

35. See David Hollenbach, *Claims in Conflict: Retrieving and Renewing the Catholic Human Rights Tradition* (New York: Paulist Press, 1979), 13–20.

36. Ibid., 20–25.

1. Men also become vulnerable to the extent they sustain the commitments implied in their reproductive behavior, but many men do not in fact sustain that commitment, either by not marrying the mothers of their children or by not taking realistic financial measures after divorce.

2. Sheila B. Kamerman and Alfred J. Kahn, *Child Care, Family Benefits, and Working Parents: A Study in Comparative Policy* (New York: Columbia University Press, 1981), 5.

3. *Planning a Family Policy for California*, first year report of the Joint Select Task Force on the Changing Family, prepared by Sherry Novick, with Joan Walsh and Elaine Zimmerman (Sacramento, Calif.: State Capitol, April 1989), 65.

4. Ibid., 22–23.

5. The 1991 statistic is derived from tables 97 and 100 of the *Statistical Abstract of the United States: 1994* (Washington, D. C.: 1994). Also see Steven D. McLaughlin, Barbara D. Melber, John O. G. Billy, Denise M. Zimmerle, Linda D. Winges, and Terry P. Johnson, *The Changing Lives of American Women* (Chapel Hill: University of North Carolina Press, 1981), 143–44.

6. Tables 97 and 100 of the *Statistical Abstract of the United States: 1994*. See also Marian Wright Edelman, *Families in Peril* (Cambridge, Mass.: Harvard University Press, 1987), 13–14; and Erik Eckholm, "Solutions on Welfare: They All Cost Money," *New York Times*, 26 July 1992, A1.

7. Edelman, *Families in Peril*, 56–57; McLaughlin et al., *Changing Lives*, 145.

8. Edelman, *Families in Peril*, 3–4. According to Edelman, the poverty rates in 1983 were 85.2 percent for young black female-headed families and 72.1 percent for young white female-headed families. For older mothers the poverty rate is 38.7 percent for white female-headed families, 58.5 percent for black ones.

9. McLaughlin et al., *Changing Lives*, 32–34.

10. Ibid.

11. Ibid., 45. 1993 figures are from table 234 of the *Statistical Abstract of the United States: 1994*.

12. Barbara R. Bergmann, *The Economic Emergence of Women* (New York: Basic Books, 1986), 114.

13. Nancy Barrett, "Women and the Economy," in *The American Woman 1987–88: A Report in Depth*, ed. Sara E. Rix (New York: Norton, 1987), 101.

14. Ibid., 125.

15. R. E. Smith, ed., *The Subtle Revolution: Women at Work* (Washington, D.C.: Urban Institute, 1979), cited in McLaughlin et al., *Changing Lives*, 101.

16. McLaughlin et al., *Changing Lives*, 125.

17. Arlie Hochschild averaged the estimates from the major studies done on time use of working fathers and working mothers and discovered that working women do housework and child care roughly fifteen hours longer each week than men. Over the course of a year, these women work an extra month of twenty-four-hour days.

Some people have attempted to establish a positive relationship between the wage gap and the leisure gap, showing that men earning more than their wives work less at home, while men earning less than their wives work more at home, but Hochschild did not find this relationship. She says that in the vast majority of households money "worked" for men, in that it excused them from housework, but not for women. Rather than the logic of the pocketbook operating in the leisure gap, there is a "balancing": "According to this principle, if men lose power over women in one way, they make up for it in another way—by avoiding the second shift. In this way, they can maintain dominance over women"(see Arlie Hochschild, *The Second Shift* [New York: Viking, 1989], 3–4, 221).

18. "The Wage Gap: Women's and Men's Earnings," Briefing Paper No. 1 for the National Committee on Pay Equity, prepared with the assistance of the Institute for Women's Policy Research, Washington, D.C., 1992. The wage gap is discussed in this source in three ways: comparing annual earnings, weekly earnings, and hourly earnings. The most familiar manner of measuring the wage gap is by annual earnings, and figures for this measure have been recorded for the longest time. Sources citing weekly and hourly earnings will show less of a wage gap. According to 1990 U.S. census data, full-time women workers earned 72 cents for every dollar earned by full-time male workers on a weekly basis; in 1993, women's hourly wages reached 78 percent of men's. The annual wage gap would be larger.

19. I saw this phenomenon, first reported by the Bureau of Labor Statistics in 1987, cited in McLaughlin et al., *Changing Lives*, 113. The phenomenon is confirmed in the briefing paper "The Wage Gap," cited above, using data through 1992. For a depiction of the life cycle of wages by gender see Roberta Spalter-Roth and Heidi Hartmann, "Raising Women's Earnings: The Family Issue of the 1990s," in *Buying America Back: Economic Choices for the 1990s*, ed. Jonathan Greenberg and William Kistler (Tulsa, Okla.: Council Oak Books, 1992), 384–95.

20. Barrett, "Women and the Economy," 130.

21. One year after a divorce or separation, adjusted family income for all women had dropped by 9 to 25 percent of its pre-divorce level (depending upon the exact method of calculation) and had risen 13 percent for men. These averages conceal large variations. The fall in living standards was much sharper for women whose families had been in the top half of the range of income: 29 percent of women from these affluent pre-divorce families had experienced a drop in adjusted income of more than half by one year after the divorce. In contrast, 19 percent of women from less affluent pre-divorce families had

comparable income drops, and 38 percent actually experienced a rise in adjusted income by one year after the divorce (see Andrew Cherlin, "Women and the Family," in Rix, *The American Woman 1987–1988*, 89).

22. This latter phenomenon is the reason many women now look askance at no-fault divorce laws. The changes in divorce laws from fault-based grounds to no-fault grounds have hurt divorced women economically. The new laws assume that husbands and wives are equals, while in reality most wives have far less earning potential than their husbands; older wives may not have worked for wages in decades, and younger, better-educated women may have worked only part-time or withdrawn from the labor force when their children were young, thus foregoing the opportunity to develop a career. Settlements that award the wife half the family's property leave the wife and children dependent on her earning power and her ex-husband's child support payments; the latter is often unreliable and quite insufficient (see Cherlin, "Women and the Family," 87–88).

23. It must also be said, particularly for the benefit of those who believe that women's participation in the labor market has resulted in broken families, that such an association is not borne out by the evidence. It is true that women who have a way of supporting themselves are less likely to put up with abuse and marital alienation than are women who are at-home workers, as Chapter 4 will describe. However, many families would be economically insolvent without women's wages. Many women keep their families together by their participation in the paid labor force.

24. *Low Wage Jobs and Workers: Trends and Options for Change*, final report to the U.S. Department of Labor (Washington, D.C.: Institute for Women's Policy Research, 1989). Another Institute study reports the premium gained for workers who are unionized: white men earn a union premium of 4.2 percent, black men 18.5 percent, Hispanic men 23.6 percent; white women 10.7 percent, black women 17.5 percent, and Hispanic women 22.0 percent, when other factors are held constant (see Roberta M. Spalter-Roth and Heidi I. Hartmann, *Women in Telecommunications: Exception to the Rule of Low Pay for Women's Work* [Washington, D.C.: Institute for Women's Policy Research, May 1992], 6).

25. Kamerman and Kahn, *Child Care*, 25. See also Roberta M. Spalter-Roth and Heidi I. Hartmann, *Dependence on Men, the Market, or the State: The Rhetoric and Reality of Welfare Reform* (Washington, D.C.: Institute for Women's Policy Research, November 1993), 5.

26. Roberta M. Spalter-Roth and Heidi I. Hartmann, *Unnecessary Losses: Costs to Americans of the Lack of Family and Medical Leave* (Washington, D.C.: Institute for Women's Policy Research, 1990), 17–19.

27. *Ways and Means* (newsletter of the National Center for Policy Alternatives, Washington, D. C.) 12, no. 2 (Summer 1989): 2.

28. Ibid.

29. Margaret A. Farley, *Personal Commitments: Beginning, Keeping, Changing* (San Francisco: Harper, 1986).

30. Readers familiar with the Boston school of personalism may recognize that I am using language here that comes from the framework of an appeal to moral law by Edgar S. Brightman and others. I want to acknowledge an ongoing conversation in which I have engaged the personalist tradition as to its relevance for reflection on economic justice for women. That tradition has been interpreted best for me by Walter G. Muelder, *Moral Law in Christian Social Ethics* (Richmond, Va.: John Knox Press; New York: Edwin Mellen, 1966).

31. Aida Torres and Jacqueline Darroch Forrest, "Why Do Women Have Abortions?" *Family Planning Perspectives*, October 1988.

32. Edelman, *Families in Peril*, 5–6.

33. "What Is Temporary Disability Insurance?" research brief (Washington, D.C.: Institute for Women's Policy Research, May 1993), 1.

34. Kamerman and Kahn, *Child Care*. Another source that used Sheila Kamerman's research, and extends her purview to include Britain and Italy, is Sylvia Ann Hewlett, *A Lesser Life: The Myth of Women's Liberation in America* (New York: Warner Books, 1986). Hewlett couches her work in terms of a criticism of the priorities of the contemporary women's movement in the United States. That agenda is not one I share, but the inclusion of Italy, primarily Roman Catholic and yet still more intentional than the United States about supporting women in the labor force with children, is instructive.

35. Kamerman and Kahn, *Child Care*. Their data is from the German Democratic Republic and the Federal Republic of Germany (before reunification), Hungary, Sweden, France, and the United States.

36. Ibid., 115. The most frequent means of covering over-threes in the other studied countries is preschool.

37. Ibid., 180–91.

38. For a good review of the uneven standards that apply to day care in the different states and a discussion of why there is an inherent contradiction in letting market forces be a major mechanism for providing child care services, see Deborah Fallows, *A Mother's Work* (Boston: Houghton Mifflin, 1985), 142–82. Fallows thinks the development of large chains of for-profit day care centers illustrates a special case of market failure: what the chains need in order to maximize profits is often incompatible with what children need in order to thrive.

39. "Statement of Jane L. Norwood, Ph.D., Commissioner, Bureau of Labor Statistics" before the House Select Committee on Children, Youth, and Families, 99th Congress, 17 April 1986.

40. Kamerman and Kahn, *Child Care*, 122.

41. Ibid.

42. Jay Belsky and Michael J. Rovine, "Nonmaternal Care in the First Year of Life and the Security of Infant-Parent Attachment," *Child Development* 59 (1988): 157–65.

43. Thomas J. Gamble and Edward Zigler, "Effects of Infant Day Care: Another Look at the Evidence," *American Journal of Orthopsychiatry* 56, no. 1 (1986): 29.

44. For instance, research published in 1985, testing a population marked by stability in the home environment unrelated to maternal employment (i.e., ruling out poverty and the instability of other family relationships) reported that maternal employment does not affect the security of attachments or the problem-solving behavior of toddlers (M. Ann Easterbrooks and Wendy A. Goldberg, "Effects of Early Maternal Employment on Toddlers, Mothers, and Fathers," *Developmental Psychology* 21, no. 5 [1985]: 774). Gamble and Zigler, however, challenge the significance of the conclusions of studies conducted on stable, middle-class families using high-quality centers.

45. Sheila B. Kamerman, "Child Care Services: An Issue for Gender Equity and Women's Solidarity," *Child Welfare* 64, no. 3 (May / June 1985): 268.

46. Gamble and Zigler take this position. So does T. Berry Brazelton, M.D., in "Issues for Working Parents," *American Journal of Orthopsychiatry* 56, no. 1 (January 1986): 23.

47. Martha S. Hill, "The Changing Nature of Poverty," *Annals of the American Academy of Political and Social Science* 479 (May 1985): 35; and "Everything Money Can Buy," *Family Affairs* 2, no. 1, (Spring 1989): 5, citing 1988 U.S. Census Bureau.

48. Hill, "The Changing Nature of Poverty," 38. Also see Diana M. Pearce, "The Feminization of Poverty: A Second Look," paper presented at the American Sociological Association meetings in San Francisco, August 1989, and circulated by the Institute for Women's Policy Research, 19.

49. Kamerman, "Child Care Services," 264.

50. Heidi I. Hartmann and Roberta M. Spalter-Roth, *The Real Employment Opportunities of Women Participating in AFDC: What the Market Can Provide* (Washington, D.C.: Institute for Women's Policy Research, October 1993), 1–10.

51. Hill, "The Changing Nature of Poverty," 47.

52. Frances A. Campbell, Bonnie Breitmayer, and Craig T. Ramey, "Disadvantaged Single Teenage Mothers and Their Children: Consequences of Free Educational Day Care" *Family Relations* 35 (1986): 63–68.

53. Hill, "The Changing Nature of Poverty," 46.

54. Advisory Committee on Social Witness Policy, *Sustainable Development, Reformed Faith, and U.S. International Economic Policy* (Louisville, Ky.: United Presbyterian Church [USA], 1994), 59.

55. In 1967, the poorest 20 percent of families with children received 6.6 percent of all income, while the richest one-fifth received 38.5 percent. In 1984, those

figures were 4.2 percent and 42.1 percent (see "The Changing Economic Circumstances of Children: Families Losing Ground," *Focus* 9, no. 9 [Spring 1986], published by the University of Wisconsin Institute for Research on Poverty, 8). Also see Spencer Rich, "Income Gap Found Wider in 43 States" *Washington Post*, 28 August 1992, A3. Rich says that in the last three years of the 1980s the average annual income nationally in 1992 dollars was $10,287 for the lowest fifth of families; it was $96,769 for the top fifth.

56. This brief historical overview is suggested to me by the "Statement of Julie A. Matthaei, Ph.D., Chair, Department of Economics, Wellesley College" before the House Select Committee on Children, Youth, and Families, 99th Congress, 17 April 1986.

57. Barrett, "Women and the Economy," 107. Also see Spalter-Roth and Hartmann, *Dependence on Men*, 4; this source used 1991 census data. I also consulted Jonathan Marshall, "Women Weathered Recession Better than Men, Data Show" *San Francisco Chronicle*, 20 August 1993, A4; this article used Labor Department statistics of July 1993, confirming these numbers.

58. Hochschild's *The Second Shift* is a rich resource of interview material on these issues with two-working-parent couples.

59. Ibid., 14.

3. SEXUAL HARASSMENT

1. For a discussion of the sexualization of work, see David L. Bradford, Alice C. Sargent, and Melinda S. Sprague, "The Executive Man and Woman: The Issue of Sexuality," in *Sexuality in Organizations: Romantic and Coercive Behaviors at Work*, ed. Gail Ann Neugarten and Jay M. Shafritz (Oak Park, Ill.: Moore, 1980), 17–28. Also see Heather Hemming, "Women in a Man's World: Sexual Harassment," *Human Relations* 38, no. 1, (1985): 67–79. Both these sources use an analysis by Rosabeth Kanter, *Men and Women of the Corporation* (New York: Basic Books, 1977).

2. Bradford, Sargent, and Sprague, "The Executive Man and Woman," 19.

3. Unless, of course, competence is defined in terms of interactive styles more typical of women. Women's interactive styles tend to be "enabling," behavior or language that supports whatever the partner is doing and keeps the interaction going, such as acknowledging another's comment or expressing agreement. Men's interactive styles tend to be "constricting" or "restricting" and to cause the partner to withdraw or shorten the interaction; such interaction involves threatening, directly contradicting or interrupting, topping the partner's story, boasting, or engaging in other forms of self-display. Males' concern for turf and dominance underlies their style and lack of self-disclosure. However, males enjoy females' responses to them much more than females

enjoy males' responses (see Eleanor E. Maccoby, "Gender and Relationships: A Developmental Account," *American Psychologist* 45, no. 4 [April 1990]: 513–20).

4. Bradford, Sargent, and Sprague, "The Executive Man and Woman," 20–24.

5. Discussions of roles and socialization are of necessity open-ended. Socialization into roles is very powerful, but clearly some social pressure to conform to roles is ineffective, since people step out of role and rebel against socialization. Therefore, socialization into roles may be a real social phenomenon without totally answering the question of causation of a given act. Eleanor E. Maccoby reminds us that social behavior is never a function of the individual alone; it is a function of the interaction between two or more persons, and individuals behave differently with different partners (see Maccoby, "Gender and Relationships," 513). The role pairs that follow can be portrayed as social phenomena, as they are here, or they may be portrayed as evidence of deep personal needs, in a theurapeutic model that may have much to offer persons who become aware of the extent to which their behavior is part of a self-destructive pattern, but have little social support or clear motivation for changing it.

6. Thanks to my colleague Marty Stortz for suggesting the name. I used the quotes to distinguish between men who are profeminist and men who haven't allowed feminism to transform their desire for dominance over women.

7. The research of N. M. Henley is cited in Hemming, "Women in a Man's World," 67–79.

8. Ibid., 72.

9. The term was coined by a group of women in a discussion class at Cornell University.

10. Peggy Crull, "Searching for the Causes of Sexual Harassment: An Examination of Two Prototypes" in *Hidden Aspects of Women's Work*, ed. Christine Bore, Roslyn Feldberg, and Natalie Sokoloff (New York, Westport, and London: Praeger, 1987), 232–35.

11. Discussed in Catharine A. MacKinnon, *Sexual Harassment of Working Women* (New Haven and London: Yale University Press, 1979), 32–33. The lawsuit is reported as *Tomkins v. Public Service Electric and Gas* Co., 422 F. Supp. 533 (D. N. J. 1977) reversed on appeal, 568 F.2d 1044 (3rd Cir. 1977).

12. For descriptions of quid pro quo and atmosphere harassment, both MacKinnon's *Sexual Harassment of Working Women*, and Crull's, "Searching for the Causes" are helpful.

13. This case is discussed in Crull, "Searching for the Causes," 228–29.

14. Cases illustrating MacKinnon's distinction are cited by Crull, ibid.

15. Katherine A. Benson describes such examples of contrapower harassment in "Comment on Crocker's 'An Analysis of University Definitions of Sexual

Harassment,'" *Signs: Journal of Women in Culture and Society* 9, no. 3 (1984): 516.

16. Crull, "Searching for the Causes," 236.

17. Ibid., 240–41.

18. This experience was confided to me after a presentation to area denominational staff members.

19. This court case is cited in Wendy Pollack, "Sexual Harassment: Women's Experience v. Legal Definitions," *Harvard Women's Law Journal*, Spring 1990, 35–85. I owe this reference to William W. May, in a paper entitled "Sexual Harassment and the Tension Between Rights and Liberties," prepared for discussion at the Business and Organizational Ethics Seminar, American Academy of Religion annual meeting, November 1992.

20. Beth E. Schneider, "Consciousness about Sexual Harassment among Heterosexual and Lesbian Women Workers," *Journal of Social Issues* 38, no. 4 (1982): 95.

21. Donald E. Maypole, "Sexual Harassment at Work: A Review of Research and Theory," *Affilia* 2, no. 1 (1987): 31.

22. See particularly, Schneider, "Consciousness about Sexual Harassment," 83; and MacKinnon, *Sexual Harassment of Working Women*, 51.

23. Schneider, "Consciousness about Sexual Harassment," 75–98. Schneider notes that lesbian and heterosexual women all receive mutual advantage from solidarity as women in the workplace. Lesbians fear the loss of their jobs if their sexual identity is known; one way men pressure heterosexual women for sexual favors is to call them lesbians if they do not comply. When "lesbian" means friend rather than outcast, all women will be more secure in the workplace.

24. Cited in *Naming the Unnamed: Sexual Harassment in the Church*, by the Council on Women and the Church (Louisville, Ky.: United Presbyterian Church [USA], 1983), 7.

25. Douglas I. McIntyre and James C. Renick, "Developing Public Policy on Sexual Harassment," *San Jose Studies* 12, no. 2 (Spring 1986): 40.

26. Edward Lafontaine and Leslie Tredeau, "The Frequency, Sources, and Correlates of Sexual Harassment among Women in Traditional Male Occupations," *Sex Roles* 15, nos. 7/8, (1986): 435–36.

27. May D. Faucher and Kenneth J. McCulloch, "Sexual Harassment in the Workplace," in Neugarten and Shafritz, *Sexuality in Organizations*, 88.

28. Lafontaine and Tredeau, "Women in Traditional Male Occupations," 435.

29. This pithy summary of the condition of sexual harassment is found in Neugarten and Shafritz, *Sexuality in Organizations*, 2.

30. Any time the word "provocative" is used to describe a woman's dress I become alert to the fact that men's attempts to "decode" the symbols of women's dress almost always seem to focus on whether or not she is communicating

sexual availability. I believe that women attempt to communicate through dress on more topics than this one, but that many of our codes are not "broken" by male interpreters.

31. Lafontaine and Tredeau, "Women in Traditional Male Occupations," 436.

32. See Gilda Berger, *Women, Work and Wages* (New York: Franklin Watts, 1986), 94. A landmark study based on data collected by the U.S. Merit Systems Protection Board in 1981 found that in the two years prior to answering the question, 42 percent of women and 15 percent of men (all working for the federal government) reported having been sexually harassed at work; a British trade union conducted a study in the city of Liverpool (published 1981) which found that 52 percent of women and 20 percent of men had experienced some form of sexual harassment, the men having been harassed by other men (M. Dawn McCaghy, *Sexual Harassment: A Guide to Resources* [Boston: G. K. Hall, 1985], 41, 30).

33. Barbara A. Gutek and Bruce Morasch, "Sex-Ratios, Sex-Role Spillover, and Sexual Harassment of Women at Work," *Journal of Social Issues* 38, no. 4 (1982): 57.

34. Laura J. Evans, "Sexual Harassment: Women's Hidden Occupational Hazard," in *The Victimization of Women*, ed. Jane Roberts Chapman and Margaret Gates (Beverly Hills, Calif.: Sage Publications, 1978), 221.

35. Mary P. Rowe, "Dealing with Sexual Harassment," *Harvard Business Review* 59, no. 3 (May–June 1981): 42–44, 46.

36. Study cited in note 32, above; Hanley cited by Neugarten and Shafritz, *Sexuality in Organizations*, 4.

37. For documentation of these economic effects of sexual harassment, see Neugarten and Shafritz, *Sexuality in Organizations*, 4; Peggy Crull, "The Impact of Sexual Harassment on the Job: A Profile of the Experiences of Ninety-Two Women," in Neugarten and Shafritz, *Sexuality in Organizations*, 70; Evans, "Hidden Occupational Hazard," 206–7; and James E. Gruber and Lars Bjorn, "Women's Responses to Sexual Harassment: An Analysis of Sociocultural, Organizational, and Personal Resource Models," *Social Science Quarterly* 67, no. 4 (1986): 817.

38. United States Merit Systems Protection Board, *Sexual Harassment in the Federal Workplace: Is It a Problem?* (Washington, D.C.: Government Printing Office, 1981).

39. In 1973, employed women averaged only 2.8 years of continuous service with the same employer, while men averaged 4.6 years (Lin Farley, *Sexual Shakedown: The Sexual Harassment of Women on the Job* [New York: McGraw-Hill, 1978], 46).

40. Ibid.

41. Walter Berns, "Terms of Endearment," *Harper's* 261, no. 1565 (October 1980).

42. I appreciate the work Bill May has done to identify the perspectives of persons favoring the civil liberties approach to sexual harassment, which he describes in his paper "Sexual Harassment and the Tension Between Rights and Liberties" (cited in note 19, above).

43. Nadine Stroessen, "Regulating Racist Speech on Campus: A Modest Proposal," *Duke Law Journal* 1990, no. 3 (June): 491–506. I thank Bill May for this reference.

44. Pamela Cooper-White, in *The Cry of Tamar: Violence against Women and the Church's Response* (Philadelphia: Augsburg-Fortress, 1994), cites this reasoning of the court for adopting the "reasonable woman" standard rather than the reasonable man standard in assessing the validity of sexual harassment claims, in the 1991 case *Ellison vs. Brady* (U.S. Court of Appeals, 9th Circuit, No. 89–15248).

45. Hemming, "Women in a Man's World," 72.

46. I cannot write the words "point persons for change" without thinking of Anita Hill and her testimony during the hearings of the Senate Judiciary Committee concerning the confirmation of Clarence Thomas as Supreme Court Justice in October 1991. The racialized response of Thomas to Hill's charges was not solely a red herring, since power is racialized in the U.S., just as it has gender associations. We are still living with the legacy of slavery, wherein black women were routinely abused and black men were emasculated in many ways, one of which was by lynching after charges of attempted rape of white women. This history provides a part of the context of all charges of sexual misconduct against African-American men and prevented gender justice for Anita Hill.

47. Rowe, "Dealing with Sexual Harassment," 42–44, 46.

48. Maypole, "Sexual Harassment at Work," 32–33.

49. I have been summarizing research conducted by Inger W. Jensen and Barbara A. Gutek, "Attributions and Assignment of Responsibility in Sexual Harassment," *Journal of Social Issues* 38, no. 4 (1982): 121–36.

50. Ibid., 134.

51. Alison M. Konrad and Barbara A. Gutek, "Impact of Work Experiences on Attitudes toward Sexual Harassment," *Administrative Science Quarterly* 31 (1986): 422–38.

4. DOMESTIC VIOLENCE

1. Coni Staff, "The Problem of Lesbian Battering," unpublished paper, 18 December 1987, 3. As Staff explains, lesbian battering takes the same forms as battering in heterosexual relationships.

2. Ann Jones, *Next Time, She'll Be Dead: Battering and How to Stop It* (Boston: Beacon, 1994), 88. Marie Fortune, Executive Director of the Center for the

Prevention of Sexual Domestic Violence, Seattle, Washington, advocates a conservative definition of abuse, limited to situations where physical violence is threatened or actual, where persons feel fear for their safety or for their very lives; she includes psychological abuse within the definition of domestic violence because psychological abuse is always in the context of the threat of physical violence (see Marie Fortune, "The Nature of Abuse," *Pastoral Psychology* 41, no. 5, [May 1993]: 276–79). The "American Medical Association Diagnostic and Treatment Guidelines on Domestic Violence," prepared by Anne H. Flitcraft, M.D., et al. (*Archives of Family Medicine* 1 [September 1992]: 39–47) also includes psychological abuse among the characteristics of domestic violence behaviors.

3. Antonia C. Novello, M.D., M. P. H., Surgeon General, U. S. Public Health Service; Mark Rosenberg, M. D., Ph.D., and Linda Saltzman, Ph.D., National Center for Environmental Health and Injury Control, Centers for Disease Control, Atlanta, Ga.; and John Shosky, Ph.D., Consultant to the Surgeon General, "From the Surgeon General, U.S. Public Health Service," *Journal of the American Medical Association* 267, no. 23 (17 June 1992): 3132.

4. R. J. Gelles, *The Violent Home* (Beverly Hills, Calif.: Sage Publications, 1974); Murray Strauss, "Wife Beating: How Common and Why?" *Victimology* 2, nos. 2–4 (1977–78): 443–58; Janet Baker Fleming, *Stopping Wife Abuse* (New York: Doubleday Anchor, 1979), 154–55. Some of the figures regarding the extent of the problem of domestic violence are estimates, since unless assault in the home is reported to law enforcement officials or physicians, what occurs behind closed doors is private and not measured for public information. Still, it is clear that a woman is more likely to suffer from physical violence in her own home at the hands of her partner than in any other situation.

5. M. A. Strauss, R. J. Gelles, and S. K. Steinmetz, *Behind Closed Doors* (New York: Anchor, 1981).

6. In addition to the Novello et al. citation above, see Nancy Kathleen Sugg, M.D., and Thomas Inui, M.D., "Primary Care Physicians' Response to Domestic Violence," *Journal of the American Medical Association* 267, no. 23 (17 June 1992): 3157.

7. "AMA Urges Questioning on Abuse," *Washington Post*, 17 June 1992, A1.

8. American Medical Association, Council on Scientific Affairs, "Violence Aginst Women: Relevance for Medical Practitioners," in *Journal of the American Medical Association* 267, no. 23 (17 June 1992): 3187.

9. Ibid., 3185–86.

10. Fortune, "The Nature of Abuse," 279.

11. "AMA Diagnostic and Treatment Guidelines," 40.

12. Staff, "The Problem of Lesbian Battering," 3.

13. Beverly Wildung Harrison, "Misogyny and Homophobia: The Unexplored Connections," in *Making the Connections: Essays in Feminist Social Ethics*, ed. Carol S. Robb (Boston: Beacon, 1985). Homophobia may be particularly virulent against gay men because the assumption is that one of the partners is "feminized"; when homophobia is directed against lesbian women, it has more to do with resistance to the idea that women can be sexually active without male penetration.

14. This argument is made by Ann Jones in *Next Time, She'll Be Dead*, 90–91. Karen Steinhauser, Chief Deputy District Attorney in the Denver District Attorney's Office, makes the same analogy (see her "Legal Issues in Sexual Abuse and Domestic Violence," *Pastoral Psychology* 41, no. 5 [May 1993]: 324).

15. Jones, *Next Time, She'll Be Dead*, 93.

16. Jean Grossholtz, "Battered Women's Shelters and the Political Economy of Sexual Violence," in *Families, Politics, and Public Policy: A Feminist Dialogue on Women and the State*, ed. Irene Diamond (New York: Longman, 1983), 64.

17. AMA Council on Scientific Affairs, "Violence Against Women," 3186.

18. Lenore E. Walker, "Treatment Alternatives for Battered Women," in *The Victimization of Women*, ed. Jane Roberts Chapman and Margaret Gates (Beverly Hills, Calif.: Sage Publications, 1978), 146–54.

19. Steinhauser, "Legal Issues," 324.

20. Susan Schechter, *Women and Male Violence: The Visions and Struggles of the Battered Women's Movement* (Boston: South End Press, 1982), 222.

21. Ibid., 212.

22. Walker, "Treatment Alternatives," 146.

23. Charlotte Germane, Margaret Johnson, and Nancy Lemon, "Mandatory Custody Mediation and Joint Custody Orders in California: The Danger for Victims of Domestic Violence," in Chapman and Gates, *The Victimization of Women*; Walker, "Treatment Alternatives."

24. Novello et al., "From the Surgeon General," 3132.

25. Julian Barling and Alan Rosenbaum, "Work Stressors and Wife Abuse," *Journal of Applied Psychology* 1, no. 2 (1986): 347; Jerry Finn, "The Stresses and Coping Behavior of Battered Women," *Social Casework: The Journal of Contemporary Social Work*, June 1985, 341; Bailing and Rosenblum, "Work Stressors and Wife Abuse," 346; Schechter, *Women and Male Violence*, 211–15.

26. Schechter, *Women and Male Violence*.

27. Sharon K. Long, Ann D. Witte, and Patrice Karr, "Family Violence: A Microeconomic Approach," *Social Science Research* 12 (1983): 363–92.

28. Murray A. Straus and Richard J. Gelles, "Societal Change and Change in Family Violence from 1975 to 1985 as Revealed by Two National Surveys," *Journal of Marriage and the Family* 48 (August 1986): 465.

29. Dorothy Q. Thomas and Michele E. Beasley, "Domestic Violence as a Human Rights Issue," *Human Rights Quarterly* 15 (1993): 44–46. This article cites the findings in 1985 of the participants at the Final Conference of the Decade for Women, in Nairobi, Kenya.

30. Elizabeth Gould Davis, *The First Sex* (Baltimore: Penguin, 1971), 257.

31. Ibid., 217.

32. L. William Countryman, *Dirt, Greed, and Sex: Sexual Ethics in the New Testament and Their Implications for Today* (Philadelphia: Fortress, 1988), 150–55.

33. Ibid., 156.

34. Lawrence Stone, *The Family, Sex, and Marriage in England 1500–1800* (New York: Harper and Row, 1977), 195.

35. Ibid., 154–55.

36. Another way to say this is that there is a gender system in the society at large and that gender system assigns responsibilities and rewards to females and males differently. The assignments have religious, psychological, social, political, and economic dimensions. Every society has a gender system. All societies have expectations about what is appropriate work for women to do, what's appropriate work for men to do, whether the boundaries are rigid or fluid, and whether or not it's appropriate to apply pressure if these boundaries are crossed. The *content* of sex role expectations varies tremendously, however, and often does not appear to depend upon anatomical differences between the sexes. Knitting, weaving, and cooking sometimes fall into the male province, while such things as pearl diving, canoe handling, and housebuilding turn out to be women's work in some settings. There are cultures in which men display such emotional qualities as sensitivity, affection, and volatile emotionality, while females are aggressive and calculating. In one culture studied by Margaret Mead, it was the male province to wear makeup and jewelry and have elaborate hairdos, and to visit with other men and gossip for extended periods of time; the women were unadorned, pragmatic, nonexpressive with each other, and spent their time working.

In every society there is also a range of shared tasks. Some societies maintain the male and female spheres rigidly separate; others permit a great deal of flexibility. Some value women's work equally with men's, and others value men's more highly; in societies that value men's more highly than women's, men will not do women's work, saying it is not worthy of them (see Sherry B. Ortner, "Is Female to Male as Nature Is to Culture?" in *Woman, Culture, and Society*, ed. Michelle Zimbalist and Louise Lamphere [Stanford: Stanford University, 1974], 67–87; and Patricia Draper, "!Kung Women: Contrasts in Sexual Egalitarianism in Foraging and Sedentary Contexts," in *Toward an Anthropology of Women*, ed. Rayna R. Reiter [New York: Monthly Review Press, 1975], 77–109).

37. Lucretia Marmon, "Domestic Violence: The Cost to Business," *Working Woman* 19, no. 4 (April 1994): 17–18.

38. Perhaps the Domestic Violence Action Committee, formed and funded by top female executives from Liz Claiborne, Reebok, and Ben & Jerry's, among other firms, will initiate this research (ibid.).

39. For a review of studies linking homelessness to domestic violence, see Joan Zorza, "Woman Battering: A Major Cause of Homelessness," *Clearinghouse Review*, special issue 1991: 421–29.

40. Jones, *Next Time, She'll Be Dead*, 209–11.

41. In the UN's *International Covenants on Human Rights*, see art. 2, para. 2, of the "International Covenant on Economic, Social and Cultural Rights," and art. 2, para. 1, of the "International Covenant on Civil and Political Rights."

42. I have benefited from the treatment of domestic violence in the context of international law, and am indebted to Thomas and Beasley, "Domestic Violence as a Human Rights Issue," 36–62.

43. Sugg and Inui, "Primary Care Physicians' Response," 3158. Sugg and Inui state, "When asked about a previous history of child abuse or physical violence with an intimate partner, 14 percent of male physicians (in 6 satellite clinics of a Seattle urban health maintenance organization) and 31 percent of female physicians acknowledged their own experience."

44. These states are California, Kentucky, Mississippi, New Hampshire, New Mexico, Pennsylvania, Rhode Island. For information regarding the complexities surrounding mandatory reporting by health care providers, contact the Family Violence Prevention Fund, San Francisco, Calif.

45. Esta Soler, Executive Director of the Family Violence Prevention Fund, is concerned that mandatory reporting could be a grave and costly mistake.

46. Steinhauser, "Legal Issues," 326

47. Ibid.

48. Conversation with San Francisco Theological Seminary student Fran Elton, 14 March 1990.

49. Teri Randall, "ACOG Renews Domestic Violence Campaign, Calls for Changes in Medical School Curricula," *Journal of the American Medical Association* 267, no. 23 (17 June 1992): 3131.

50. Joyce Gelb, "The Politics of Wife Abuse," in Diamond, *Families, Politics, and Public Policy*, 250–62.

51. Ibid., 257.

52. Donna Chavis, of the Fellowship of Reconciliation, described this effort on the part of the Rosebud Sioux in a workshop at the Women's Interseminary Conference, San Anselmo, Calif., 10 March 1990.

53. Straus and Gelles, "Societal Change," 473.

5. LESBIAN IDENTITY

1. Evelyn Blackwood, "Breaking the Mirror: The Construction of Lesbianism and the Anthropological Discourse on Homosexuality," *Journal of Homosexuality* 11, nos. 3 / 4 (1986): 1–17.

2. Ibid., 10.

3. The overall perspective here is informed by Blackwood's research. However, it is corroborated by Alan Bell and Martin Weinberg, whose research found more heterosexuality in the behaviors and feelings of the homosexual women they studied than in gay male counterparts. Lesbians' ratings of themselves on the Kinsey Scale were less apt to agree with their actual sexual histories than were those of the males, suggesting that the women were less likely to behave sexually in accordance with their true interests. Bell and Weinberg wonder whether lesbians' greater heterosexuality simply reflects a history of accommodation to males in a sexual context and / or conformity to societal expectations (see Alan P. Bell and Martin S. Weinberg, *Homosexualities: A Study of Diversity among Men and Women* [New York: Simon and Schuster, 1978], 60).

4. Blackwood documents the past existence of "sisterhoods" in Kwangtung province, China (where silk work was available), within which some women were celibate and others formed lesbian relations. On Carriacou, in the Caribbean, while males migrate to industrial areas for wage labor, their wives in their absence relate to younger women, often single, and support them with the income sent from the husband (see Blackwood, "Breaking the Mirror," 11–13). The Beguines, in fourteenth-century Europe, were women who held property or had skills and formed communities for themselves independent of male involvement.

5. The Kinsey research cited here is reported in Alfred C. Kinsey, Wardell B. Pomeroy, and Clyde E. Martin, *Sexual Behavior in the Human Male* (Philadelphia: W. B. Saunders, 1948), and in Alfred C. Kinsey, Wardell B. Pomeroy, Clyde E. Martin, and Paul H. Gebhard, *Sexual Behavior in the Human Female* (Philadelphia: W. B. Saunders, 1953). It is widely referred to in texts about human sexuality, such as Robert T. Francoeur, *Becoming a Sexual Person* (New York: John Wiley and Sons, 1982), particularly chapter 11; Joann S. DeLora, Carol A. B. Warren, and Carol Rinkleib Ellison, *Understanding Sexual Interaction* (Boston: Houghton Mifflin, 1981), particularly chapter 13; Gilbert D. Nass and Mary Pat Fisher, *Sexuality Today* (Boston: Jones and Bartlett, 1984), particularly chapter 7.

6. DeLora, Warren, and Ellison, *Understanding Sexual Interaction*, 389.

7. Bell and Weinberg, *Homosexualities*, 53.

8. Ibid., 186–87.

9. Christine Browning, "Changing Theories of Lesbianism: Challenging the Stereotypes," in *Women-Identified Women*, ed. Trudy Darty and Sandee Potter (Palo Alto: Mayfield, 1984), 11.

10. Gary David Comstock, *Violence against Lesbians and Gay Men* (New York: Columbia University Press, 1991), 109.

11. Roberta Achtenberg, *Preserving and Protecting the Families of Lesbians and Gay Men* (San Francisco: National Center for Lesbian Rights, 1990), 6.

12. What constitutes a domestic partnership may vary from locality to locality. The basic criteria usually include that each person be the sole, primary, or principal partner of the other, that they have the capacity to contract, that they live together and share responsibilities for basic living expenses. Usually domestic partnerships are recognitions that the partners would marry if the law allowed, though there is no consensus among gay men and lesbian women about the desirability of adopting marriage, modeled after the patriarchal heterosexual household, by lesbians and gays (see *Recognizing Lesbian and Gay Families: Strategies for Obtaining Domestic Partners Benefits* [San Francisco: National Center for Lesbian Rights, 1992], 17–21).

13. For a discussion of the bases for domestic partner benefits, see *Recognizing Lesbian and Gay Families*, 2–3.

14. Ibid., 2.

15. Achtenberg, *Families of Lesbians and Gay Men*, 9.

16. These are the findings of California's Joint Select Task Force on the Changing Family, *Planning a Family Policy for California*, first year report, prepared by Sherry Novick with Joan Walsh and Elaine Zimmerman (Sacramento, Calif.: State Capitol, April 1989), 100.

17. For a thorough description of the kinds of violence lesbians and gay men experience, as well as a description of the perpetrators of that violence, see Comstock, *Violence against Lesbians and Gay Men*.

18. Ibid., 36–53.

19. See Barbara Sang, "Lesbian Relationships: A Struggle toward Partner Equality," in Darty and Potter, *Women-Identified Women*; Jeannine Gramick, "Developing a Lesbian Identity," in the same volume; Jack H. Hedblom, "Dimensions of Lesbian Sexual Experience," *Archives of Sexual Behavior* 2, no. 4 (December 1973); 329–41; and Joyce C. Albro and Carol Tully, "A Study of Lesbian Lifestyles in the Homosexual Micro-Culture and the Heterosexual Macro-Culture," *Journal of Homosexuality* 4, no. 4 (Summer 1979).

20. Virginia R. Brooks, *Minority Stress and Lesbian Women* (Lexington, Mass.: Lexington Books, 1981), 62. Brooks found 28.3 percent of lesbians and 3.0 percent of heterosexual women had advanced education or professional degrees. She was using 1975 census data for this report, and found that the number of lesbians who had completed at least one college degree was 44 percent, compared with 10 percent of the general adult female population. She com-

pared this finding to another regarding men, in which 42 percent of homosexual men, versus 11.7 percent in the general census group, were college graduates. (Fifteen years later, the percentage of the general population, both women and men, who have finished a college degree is 14.5 percent, and the corresponding percentage for both lesbians and gay men is probably much higher.)

21. Hilda Hidalgo, "The Puerto Rican Lesbian in the United States," in Darty and Potter, *Women-Identified Women*, 108.

22. Ibid.

23. Beth Schneider, "Peril and Promise: Lesbians' Workplace Participation," in Darty and Potter, *Women-Identified Women*, 213.

24. Ibid., 211–12.

25. Ibid., 221.

26. Hidalgo, "The Puerto Rican Lesbian," 109.

27. Schneider, "Peril and Promise," 214.

28. Ibid., 223.

29. Dominick Vetri, "The Legal Arena: Progress for Gay Civil Rights," *Journal of Homosexuality* 5, nos. 1 / 2 (Fall 1979 / Winter 1980): 30.

30. Martin P. Levine and Robin Leonard, "Discrimination Against Lesbians in the Work Force," in *The Lesbian Issue: Essays from Signs*, ed. Estelle B. Freedman, Barbara C. Gelpi, Susan L. Johnson, and Kathleen M. Weston (Chicago: University of Chicago Press, 1985), 190–91.

31. Ibid.

32. Sang, "Lesbian Relationships," 56–59.

33. Ibid., 31. By 1980, twenty-one states had legislatively ended the criminalization of consensual sodomy by adults in private.

34. Chart prepared by the Lambda Legal Defense and Education Fund, New York, N. Y., "Sodomy Laws State-by-State as of August 1994."

35. Comstock, *Violence against Lesbians and Gay Men*, 123.

36. This background to *Bowers v. Hardwick* is recounted in Richard D. Mohr, *A More Perfect Union: Why Straight America Must Stand Up for Gay Rights* (Boston: Beacon, 1994), 19.

37. These states are California, Colorado, Connecticut, Hawaii, Illinois, Louisiana, Maryland, Massachusetts, Michigan, Minnesota, New Jersey, New Mexico, Ohio, Pennsylvania, Rhode Island, Vermont, Washington, and Wisconsin. A bill was introduced in Congress in June 1994 (in the Senate by Senator Edward M. Kennedy and in the House by congressmen Barney Frank and Gerry Studds) that would prohibit employment discrimination on the basis of sexual orientation. It's called ENDA, the Employment Non-Discrimination Act of 1994, and contains exemptions for religious employers and the military.

38. *Lesbian, Gay, and Bisexual Civil Rights in the United States* (Washington, D.C.: National Gay and Lesbian Task Force Policy Institute, February 1994).

39. Bell and Weinberg, *Homosexualities*, 14.

40. Celia Kitzinger, *The Social Construction of Lesbianism* (London, Beverly Hills: Sage Publications, 1987), 46.

41. The different tendencies within feminist politics are a matter for serious study, and I do not attempt it here. For a description of the cultural feminist tendency from a critical perspective, see Alice Echols, "The Taming of the Id: Feminist Sexual Politics, 1968–83," in *Pleasure and Danger: Exploring Female Sexuality*, ed. Carole S. Vance (London: Pandora, 1992), 50–72. Celia Kitzinger (*The Social Construction of Lesbianism*) is the cultural feminist I cite in this particular section. U. S. feminists may be more familiar with Mary Daly's work within this perspective (see particularly her books *Gyn/Ecology* [Boston: Beacon, 1978] and *Pure Lust* [Boston: Beacon, 1984]).

42. These assertions served Kitzinger in her research to identify lesbians with a radical feminist political perspective (see *The Social Construction of Lesbianism*, 165).

43. Frederick L. Whitam and Robin M. Mathy, *Male Homosexuality in Four Societies* (New York: Praeger, 1986), 181.

44. Comstock, *Violence against Lesbians and Gay Men*, 123.

45. Enrique Rueda, *The Homosexual Network* (Old Greenwich, Conn.: Devin Adair Company, 1982), 200.

46. L. William Countryman, *Dirt, Greed, and Sex: Sexual Ethics in the New Testament and Their Implications for Today* (Philadelphia: Fortress, 1988).

47. Ibid., 26.

48. Victor Paul Furnish, "The Bible and Homosexuality: Reading the Texts in Context," in *Homosexuality in the Church: Both Sides of the Debate*, ed. Jeffrey S. Siker (Louisville, Ky.: Westminster John Knox Press, 1994), 20.

49. Countryman, *Dirt, Greed, and Sex*, 86.

50. Ibid., 108.

51. Ibid., 117.

52. Ibid., 244.

53. The term "dynamic analogy" is Marvin Chaney's.

54. Everyone who attempts to use the Bible as authority for moral reflection uses some kind of criteria for selection of the texts. This is unavoidable, though not everyone is able to identify and articulate what their ethical criteria are. Herman Waetjen says it this way: "The laws of the Hebrew Scriptures continue to be authoritative when they are interpreted and applied according to their original divine intention, namely to establish community, communication and communion. That encompasses the termination of all forms and forces of exclusiveness and exclusion and the development of solidarity that

unites all of humanity in the pursuit of a world that nurtures justice, equality and wholeness for all people." On this basis, he reads the Pauline texts in the light of a criticism of the pollution system that dualistically separates the clean from the unclean, heterosexual from homosexual. Paul in the contemporary period would phrase Galatians 3:28 this way: "In Christ there is neither Jew nor Greek, neither slave nor free, neither heterosexual nor homosexual, neither male nor female" (Herman C. Waetjen, "Homosexuality and the Bible," presentation to the San Bernadino Presbytery, August 1994, circulated by that presbytery thereafter).

55. See Richard B. Hays, "Awaiting the Redemption of Our Bodies: The Witness of Scripture Concerning Homosexuality," in Siker, *Homosexuality in the Church.*

56. Donna Hitchens, "Social Attitudes, Legal Standards, and Personal Trauma in Child Custody Cases," *Journal of Homosexuality* 5, nos. 1/2 (Fall 1979– Winter 1980): 90. Information about the jurisdictions that are likely to view lesbian and gay identity as relevant to the well-being of children in custody disputes is available from the National Center for Lesbian Rights, San Francisco, Calif. According to the Fall 1994 NCLR Newsletter, the circuit court of Henrico County, Virginia, in September 1993 awarded custody of three-year-old Tyler Doustou to his grandmother, Kay Bottoms, who said the boy would be harmed if he were to be returned to his mother, Sharon Bottoms, and her lover, April Wade. The Virginia Court of Appeals ruled on 21 June 1994 that the trial court's antigay decision was not supported by Virginia law: "The evidence fails to prove that Sharon Bottoms, the child's mother, abused or neglected her son, that her lesbian relationship with April Wade has or will have a deleterious effect on her son, or that she is an unfit mother. To the contrary, the evidence showed that Sharon Bottoms has been a fit and nurturing parent who has adequately provided and cared for her son" (NCRL Newsletter, Fall 1994). Kay Bottom's attorney filed a petition for appeal with the Virginia Supreme Court. The Virginia Supreme Court refused on 21 April 1995 to award Sharon Bottoms custody of her son, ruling that "active lesbianism practiced in the home" could stigmatize the child (*San Francisco Chronicle,* 22 April 1995, A3).

57. Deborah Goleman Wolf, *The Lesbian Community* (Berkeley: University of California Press, 1979), 142.

58. Charlotte J. Patterson, "Children of Lesbian and Gay Parents," *Child Development* 63 (1992): 1026.

59. Achtenberg, *Families of Lesbians and Gay Men,* 2.

60. Hitchens, "Child Custody Cases," 90–91.

61. Meredith Gould, "Lesbians and the Law: Where Sexism and Heterosexism Meet," in Darty and Potter, *Women-Identified Women,* 167. Also see Nass and Fisher, *Sexuality Today,* 174.

62. A review of the relevant research and a summary of the findings on children of gay and lesbian parents is provided by Patterson, "Children of Lesbian and Gay Parents," 1025–42.

63. Vetri, "The Legal Arena," 30–31.

64. See Andreas Kincses Oberstone and Harriet Sukoneck, "Psychological Adjustment and Life Style of Single Lesbians and Single Heterosexual Women," *Psychology of Women Quarterly* 1, no. 2 (Winter 1976): 185–86.

6. SEXUAL ETHICS

1. Beverly Wildung Harrison, *Making the Connections: Essays in Feminist Social Ethics*, ed. Carol S. Robb (Boston: Beacon, 1985), 149.

2. James B. Nelson, *Embodiment: An Approach to Sexuality and Christian Theology* (Minneapolis: Augsburg, 1978), 93–97.

3. Harrison, *Making the Connections*, 149.

4. Ibid., 87.

5. Ibid., 147.

6. Ibid., 137; Nelson, *Embodiment*, 58.

7. Harrison, *Making the Connections*, 149.

8. Ibid.

9. Ibid., 18.

10. Margaret A. Farley, R. S. M., "New Patterns of Relationship: Beginnings of a Moral Revolution," in *Woman: New Dimensions*, ed. Walter J. Burghardt, S.J. (New York: Paulist Press, 1976), 67–70.

11. Harrison, *Making the Connections*, 150; Nelson, *Embodiment*, 128.

12. Beverly Wildung Harrison, *Our Right to Choose: Toward a New Ethic of Abortion* (Boston: Beacon, 1983), 106.

13. Farley, "New Patterns," 58.

14. Margaret A. Farley, "The Church and the Family: An Ethical Task," *Horizons* 10, no. 1 (1983): 63.

15. Ibid., 62.

16. Nelson, *Embodiment*, 127.

17. Margaret A. Farley, "An Ethic for Same-Sex Relations," in *A Challenge to Love: Gay and Lesbian Catholics in the Church*, ed. R. Nugent (New York: Crossroads, 1983), 101; Nelson, *Embodiment*, 126; Harrison, *Making the Connections*, 90.

18. Farley, "The Church and the Family," 61.

19. In this connection see Marge Berer, "More Than Just Saying No: What Would a Feminist Population Policy Be Like?" and the responses from a panel of theologians and family planning experts (particularly Mary Hunt's), in *Conscience: A Newsjournal of Prochoice Catholic Opinion* 12, no. 5 (September/ October 1991): 1–7.

20. Betsy Hartmann, *Reproductive Rights and Wrongs: The Global Politics of Population Control and Contraceptive Choice* (Boston: South End Press, 1995).

21. Statistics from *For Ourselves, Our Families, and Our Future: The Struggle for Childbearing Rights*, by the Childbearing Rights Information Project, ed. Marian McDonald (Boston: Red Sun Press, undated), 19. For one excellent treatment of this perspective on procreative choice, see Harrison, *Making the Connections*, 132, and her *Our Right to Choose*.

22. These criteria for evaluating sexual ethics are articulated by Christine E. Gudorf, in "Honesty and Responsibility in Teaching Sexual Ethics," paper presented at the Society for Christian Ethics, January 1991, Culver City, Calif.

23. This discussion of the importance of teaching girls how to engage in conflict is an insight that emerged in conversation with a group of Presbyterian women administrators and faculty on 20 November 1992. We were particularly noting the extent to which adolescents receive their cues for morality from their peer groups, and the difficulty of asking them to make decisions about what they do today in a way consistent with a life plan they have chosen; the adolescent period is not marked by much awareness of the future.

24. Walter G. Muelder, *Moral Law in Christian Social Ethics* (Philadelphia: John Knox; Lewiston, N.Y.: Edwin Mellen, 1966), 94–97. According to Muelder, in America personalism was formulated in the early twentieth century by Borden Parker Bowne and developed by E. S. Brightman, A. C. Knudson, R. T. Flewelling, L. Harold DeWolf, and others, including Muelder himself. "In these thinkers theism and natural theology are closely related, and have theological affinities with Christian evangelical liberalism, being critical of fundamentalism and of irrationalism in neo-orthodoxy." Personalism, broadly conceived, has several types; personal realism, personal idealism, and panpsychic idealism among them. The moral laws described and developed by Walter Muelder are the social ethics component of personal idealism (the Boston tradition), characteristic of the philosophers and theologians who have taught at Boston University. Some characteristics of this theological ethic include an interdisciplinary perspective, preference for a system of regulative moral laws in contrast to deontological cultural prescriptions, and insistence on the dialectical unity of theory and practice. In addition, a person is perceived as a socius with a private center, meaning social in nature, yet having the freedom to choose among given possibilities. Personalism thus avoids individualism. For more description of personalism, see Walter Muelder, "Per-

sonalism," in *The Westminster Dictionary of Christian Ethics*, ed. James F. Childress and John Macquarrie (Philadelphia: Westminster Press, 1986), 469–70.

25. Ibid., 96.

26. See Ramon G. McLeod, "Polluting the Globe with People," *San Francisco Chronicle*, 20 March 1992, A12.

27. Jodi L. Jacobson, *Women's Reproductive Health: The Silent Emergency*, Worldwatch Paper 102 (Washington, D.C.: Worldwatch Institute, June 1991), 52.

28. Jodi L. Jacobson, *The Global Politics of Abortion*, Worldwatch Paper 97 (Washington, D.C.: Worldwatch Institute, July 1990), 34.

29. Ibid.

30. Ibid.

31. Frances Moore Lappe and Rachel Schurman, *Taking Population Seriously* (San Francisco: Institute for Food and Development Policy, 1990), 29. However, another source indicates this percentage may be higher. Sharon Camp, Senior Vice President of Population Action International, used data from seventy developing countries and finds that organized family planning programs account for about 40 to 50 percent of the birthrate declines in those countries (see her "Global Population Stabilization: A 'No Regrets' Strategy," in *Conscience*, 14, no. 3 (Autumn 1993): 7–8.

32. Lappe and Schurman, *Taking Population Seriously*, 25–26.

33. Paul R. Ehrlich and Anne H. Ehrlich, *The Population Explosion* (New York: Simon and Schuster, 1991), 215.

34. Ibid., 216.

35. Ibid.

36. Jodi L. Jacobson, *Gender Bias: Roadblock to Sustainable Development*, Worldwatch Paper 110 (Washington, D.C.: Worldwatch Institute, September 1992), 8–9.

37. Particularly in Harrison, *Our Right to Choose*.

38. "Survey data around the world indicate that if all those who wanted to use modern contraception in fact had access to the services that would enable them to manage their sexuality and fertility safely and effectively, then the lower-level population projects might in fact be borne out. That is to say, meeting men's and women's own priorities, in the ways in which they would like them to be met, would reconcile private and public interest without recourse to draconian controls" (Janice Jiggins, "Don't Waste Energy on Fear of the Future," *Conscience* 14, no. 3, [Autumn 1993]: 29).

39. Some Protestant denominations, such as the United Methodists, have cautioned their members to be concerned about population increase in developed

and developing nations, yet they have not done what they can to "shift away from the notion that the central metaphors for divine blessing are expressed at the biological level" in births (Harrison, *Making the Connections,* 119).

40. The Presbyterians' Committee on Human Sexuality submitted its report, *Keeping Body and Soul Together: Sexuality, Spirituality, and Social Justice,* to the 1991 General Assembly of the Presbyterian Church (USA); the General Assembly voted not to adopt the report, nor the minority report, and to study the matter for three more years. The first draft of *The Church and Human Sexuality: A Lutheran Perspective,* was released by the Division for Church in Society in October 1993, to be met with much resistance.

41. One of the earliest sources on object relations theory and social power dynamics is Nancy Chodorow, *The Reproduction of Mothering* (Berkeley: University of California Press, 1978).

42. For an excellent introduction to some of the literature reflecting the work of profeminist men on the topic of violence against women, see Marvin M. Ellison, "Refusing to Be 'Good Soldiers': An Agenda for Men," in *Redefining Social Ethics,* ed. Susan E. Davies and Eleanor H. Haney (Cleveland: Pilgrim, 1991), 189–98; and Marvin M. Ellison, "Holding Up Our Half of the Sky: Male Gender Privilege as Problem and Resource for Liberation Ethics," *Journal of Feminist Studies in Religion* 9, nos. 1/2, (Spring–Fall 1993): 95–113.

43. James B. Nelson, in *The Intimate Connection: Male Sexuality, Masculine Spirituality* (Philadelphia: Westminster, 1988), builds on this theme and deepens the understanding of the positive values of men's spiritualities.

44. Gerard Fourez, *Liberation Ethics* (Philadelphia: Temple University, 1982), 111.

7. ECONOMIC ETHICS

1. See Marilyn Waring, *If Women Counted: A New Feminist Economics* (San Francisco: Harper, 1988), particularly chapter 4.

2. Specifically, consumption theory postulates homogenization, egocentricity, maximization, and comparability in family decisions about resources (see *Reforming Economics: Calvinist Studies on Methods and Institutions,* ed. John Tiemstra, with W. Fred Graham, Gerge N. Monsma, Jr., Carl J. Sinke, Alan Storkey, and a contribution by Daniel M. Ebels [Lewiston, N.Y.; Queenston, Ontario: Edwin Mellen Press, 1990], 134).

3. Ibid.

4. Vandana Shiva, *Staying Alive: Women, Ecology, and Development* (London: Zed, 1989), 40–41.

5. Iris Marion Young, *Justice and the Politics of Difference,* (Princeton, N.J.: Princeton University Press, 1990), 51.

6. Barbara Bergmann has an interesting economic analysis of the reason husbands do not participate more fully in housework. She says power in any relationship tends to flow to the partner who can most easily replace the other. It is much easier, she says, for the husband to replace the family-care services of the wife than for the wife to replace the financial contributions of the husband; when women make repeated requests for a change in the sharing of housework, men may in return threaten to leave. The disparity in economic power between men and women is one reason why at least one-quarter of working couples in the United States expect the wife will not only work full-time in the paid labor force, but do all the housework as well (Bergmann, *The Economic Emergence of Women* [New York: Basic Books, 1986], 269–70).

7. Jodi L. Jacobson, *Gender Bias: Roadblock to Sustainable Development*, Worldwatch Paper 110 (Washington, D.C.: Worldwatch Institute, September 1992), 9–19.

8. The introductory remarks of the economic justice document adopted by the Lutheran Church in America in 1980 are the source of this quote, and served as my inspiration for the whole paragraph (see *Economic Justice: Stewardship of Creation in Human Community*, distributed by the Division for Mission in North America, Lutheran Church in America, New York, N.Y., 1). The Lutheran Church in America is a predecessor body to the Evangelical Lutheran Church in America.

9. *Rerum Novarum* 19; one translation of *Rerum Novarum* is contained in *Contemporary Catholic Social Teaching* (Washington, D.C.: National Conference of Catholic Bishops, 1991), 15–43. The Lutheran Church in America's 1980 statement, *Economic Justice*, uses similar language: "Private property is not an absolute human right but is always conditioned by the will of God and the needs of the community. The obligation to serve justifies the right to possess. The creator does not sanction the accumulation of economic power and possessions as ends in themselves" (page 7). Earlier in the document economic justice is said to include accountability: "Accountability implies that economic actors must be held answerable to the community for the consequences of their behavior. Government properly establishes the legal means whereby people may secure compensation for injury incurred as a result of economic decisions which have not taken account of their likely impact on personal and community well-being."

Likewise, "The Social Principles of the United Methodist Church," adopted in 1972, contains the statement "We believe private ownership of property is a trusteeship under God, both in those societies where it is encouraged and where it is discouraged, but is limited by the overriding needs of society. We believe that Christian faith denies to any person or group of persons exclusive and arbitrary control of any other part of the created universe" ("Social Principles," part 73. IV. A, in *The Book of Resolutions of the United Methodist Church* [Nashville: United Methodist Publishing House, 1992]).

10. Readers will not find reference to the social mortgage in Presbyterian documents, but in the 1985 document *Toward a Just, Caring, and Dynamic Political Economy* one finds the following: "Yet if we think about it carefully, we see that we have not achieved our successes solely on our own. Most of us received quality education paid for by our local governments, quality that does not exist in many school districts in urban slums and rural backwaters. Many of us paid less than our full college tuition. And even if we paid full tuition, those payments did not cover the full cost of our education. Many of us have inherited a headstart from our parents. In a larger sense, we have all benefited from living in a democratic society that others have built, fought for, and even died for. At the same time that we give thanks for these benefits, we need to rededicate ourselves to giving more to others than has been given to us" (*Toward a Just, Caring, and Dynamic Political Economy*, report of the Committee on a Just Political Economy, Advisory Council on Church and Society, Presbyterian Church [USA], 15).

11. While the Presbyterians do not use the phrase "principle of subsidiarity," it is clearly the content of their discussion of the appropriate role for voluntary associations vis-a-vis government and the private sector. In *Toward a Just, Caring, and Dynamic Political Economy* we find the following: "A just political economy entails even much more than the combined efforts of the public and private sectors. It also relies on voluntary action, or the activity of the third sector—the voluntary associations. . . . When government dominates the entire political economy it crushes free and spontaneous cultural life, obliterates social experiments, and restricts the open exploration of new and different possibilities. . . . Voluntary associations cannot assume the duties and responsibilities that are legitimately those of government, however" (page 11).

12. U.S. Conference of Catholic Bishops, *Economic Justice for All* (1986 pastoral letter), section 91. The Lutheran Church in America's statement *Economic Justice* states that economic justice includes the elements of equity, accessibility, accountability, and efficiency (page 5). Accessibility is treated much as participation: "Accessibility includes both the formal entitlements (e.g., nutrition, shelter, health care, basic education, minimum income and/or employment) as are needed for entrance into the social and economic community. It also includes the provision of the means by which members of a community may participate in decisions which affect the quality of common life and that of future generations."

13. *Rerum Novarum* 14.

14. The positioning of an allowance for inequality alongside special concern for the poor is stark in the Lutheran Church in America's *Economic Justice*. Defining further how equity is required by justice, the statement says, "Understood as equity or fairness, economic justice does not mean economic equality. It is rather the result of a discerning of, and response to, the various needs of the members of a society, respecting differences without being partial to

power or special interest. Equity implies a sense of the common good and a care for the diversity of gifts and human resources that contribute to it. At the same time it provides for those *minimal necessities which, in a given social and cultural setting, are prerequisites for participation in society*; and it provides for those members of the society who, because of circumstances not of their making, cannot provide for themselves" (page 6, emphasis mine). Note the continuity of this definition of equity with the definition of human rights used by David Hollenbach and Beverly Harrison.

15. For an interesting discussion of egalitarianism and whether it is consistent with Calvin and/or the Reformed Tradition, see *Reformed Faith and Economics*, ed. Robert L. Stivers (Lanham, Md.: University Press of America, 1989), particularly Christian T. Iosso, "Reformed Economic Ethics of John Calvin," and David Little, "Economic Justice and the Ground for a Theory of Progressive Taxation in Calvin's Thought."

16. Prentiss L. Pemberton and Daniel Rush Finn, *Toward a Christian Economic Ethic* (Minneapolis: Winston Press, 1985), 36–40.

17. I am indebted to Christopher Ocker for pointing out to me the work of Peter Blickle in *The Revolution of 1525: The German Peasants' War from a New Perspective* (Baltimore and London: Johns Hopkins University Press, 1981), particularly 137–61.

18. See *The Book of Resolutions of the United Methodist Church, 1992* (Nashville: United Methodist Publishing House, 1992), where the social principles of Methodism are published, particularly regarding rights of women (page 40).

19. For statements relating to equity, see the Lutheran Church in America, *Economic Justice*, 6; and *Resolutions of the United Methodist Church, Economic Justice*, 404. The latter resolution, passed in 1988, presents a more complicated picture than my statement may suggest, in that it is stated that the covenant, including the provisions for the jubilee, grounds contemporary claims to justice. "Covenant people are committed to *equitable* distribution of resources to meet basic needs and to social systems that provide ongoing access to those resources [italics mine]." However, Israel broke its covenant with God during the period of the kings, "when the people began to turn away from Yahweh to patterns of idolatry, greed, privilege, materialism, and oppressive power." As a result of breaking the covenant, "the economic system of the community was *no longer based on equality* and concern for those who were powerless in the community but on economic privilege to the benefit of the rich and powerful" (pages 331–32, italics mine). The statement seems to conflate equity with equality, which blunts the potential power of this meaning of justice.

With regard to the concept of fairness, see the Presbyterian Church's *Toward a Just, Caring, and Dynamic Political Economy*, 10: "A just political economy does not imply equality of income, even if a democratic society promises equality before the law. Rather, justice in the political economy suggests a more indefinite condition, that of fairness. There is biblical warrant for fairness; the prophetic cry is for fair—not equal—treatment. It demands provision of basic needs of food, clothing, health care and shelter—the elimination of arbitrary blocks to providing for one's self and one's own. The issue is not the gaps between the rich and the poor, but the size of the gaps. Are they widening or narrowing? Are the current differences growing worse? What is their cumulative impact? Are the differences working for the benefit of all people or to the detriment of some? According to our view of justice, inequalities are morally unacceptable unless they can be shown to work for the benefit of all people in society." This treatment of justice as fairness shows the influence of John Rawls as much as or more than "biblical warrants."

20. Bergmann, *The Economic Emergence of Women*, 133.

21. Some colleagues believe I'm too hard on market forces here. The counterexample I'm offered is that of large corporations who have added in-house child care centers as a benefit for their employees. Let us be clear that those corporations are not in the business of child care. In fact, they usually subsidize the costs of employees' child care expenses precisely because these costs would otherwise be prohibitive for their own employees. Large corporations who offer child care subsidies to employees cover a small percentage of children needing such care, and their motivation is to reduce their employee turnover, not to compete in the child care business. As long as they believe they receive a competitive advantage by providing this benefit, they will continue to provide it. But should they conclude there is no clear change in productivity of their employees because of child care benefits corporations will very conceivably drop the benefit.

However, the market may still be *used* to provide child care. If the state of California (to use a wild example) were to offer vouchers for child care to parents of two-, three-, and four-year-olds that by legislation could only be redeemed at centers that maintained a ratio of one care giver per three children, where all staff had minimally an M. A. in early childhood education, and that limited their enrollment to twenty-four children, the market for such centers would thereby be stimulated, which would no doubt result in much more availability of centers meeting these standards.

22. I have been influenced here by Herman E. Daly and John B. Cobb, Jr., *For the Common Good: Redirecting the Economy toward Community, the Environment, and a Sustainable Future* (Boston: Beacon, 1989), chapter 11. Also see Gar Alperovitz and Jeff Faux, *Rebuilding America* (New York: Pantheon, 1984), who make the point that community integrity and stability require national planning, not local isolationism. Rather than leave planning covert and denying it is done, which is what the government currently does in piecemeal accomodations to large business, Alperovitz and Faux suggest a planning commission that has the power to coordinate the strategic flow of capital but is accountable to the political process. They recommend such a planning commission be maintained in the executive branch and its work reviewed by an

agency of the Congress; at the same time, local communities must develop their own planning process, which will feed information up through regional levels to the national level. There is prior experience in some localities to build on in this regard (see Alperovitz and Faux, particularly chapter 15). For a review of the positions against and favoring more national planning for the economy, see Daniel Rush Finn, "Ethical Dimensions of the Debate on Economic Planning," in *Catholic Social Teaching and the U.S. Economy*, ed. John W. Houck and Oliver Williams (Washington, D.C.: University Press of America, 1984), 399–443.

23. Two people who have used sector analysis in relation to the effects of the economy on women are Marilyn Waring (*If Women Counted*) and Barbara Bergmann (*The Economic Emergence of Women*).

24. I have used as my primary source for this description of energy systems the work of Amory B. Lovins and L. Hunter Lovins, *Brittle Power: Energy Strategy for National Security* (Andover, Mass.: Brick House Publishing, 1982), 43–219.

25. Ibid., 222.

26. Ibid., 267.

27. Alperovitz and Faux, *Rebuilding America*, 189.

28. There are good reasons why people in the United States are genuinely of divided opinion over the value of decentralization in the economy. Advocates and detractors associate decentralization with a refocus on small and mid-size cities in closer relationship with rural sources of food and fiber. Some are fearful of the social consequences of such a refocusing. For instance, Iris Marion Young says such ideals of community under the rubric of local autonomy reproduce the dynamics of exclusion; they are fueled by an urge to unity, experienced as shared subjectivity, which is threatened by efforts of subjugated groups to move toward empowerment. She constructs instead a normative ideal of city life, and by city life she means a form of social relations which brings together strangers. In this ideal, groups do not stand in relations of inclusion and exclusion, but overlap and intermingle without becoming homogeneous. Cities support a diversity of uses of public spaces and make possible the pleasure and excitement of being drawn out of one's secure routine to encounter the novel and strange. The city provides, or should in her view, public squares where we as people can see each other in our differentness, learn to appreciate or at least tolerate each other, and also debate the meaning of social justice (see Young, "City Life and Difference," *Justice and the Politics of Difference*). This was certainly my own experience of city life, moving as I did from rural town to mid-size city and then to urban life. The pettiness of rural communities provides a major motivation for urbanization. I believe, however, that the people of the United States have yet to develop a historical analysis of the process by which urban-rural relationships have been constructed by federal agricultural policy to move people off the land to put them in closer proximity to factories and allow consolidation of landholdings for

agribusiness. Much of what we know now as rural culture is a colonized culture. When cities' advocates also begin to advocate reinvestment in the heartland's small and medium-sized farms, education and health care for rural people, and a closer relationship of city life to its food sources, I will decrease my own concern over city elitism, born of de facto colonialism.

29. Daly and Cobb, *For the Common Good*.

30. See Herman E. Daly, "A Biblical Economic Principle and the Steady-State Economy," in *Covenant for a New Creation; Ethics, Religion, and Public Policy*, ed. Carol S. Robb and Carl J. Casebolt (Maryknoll, N.Y.: Orbis and Graduate Theological Union, 1991), 47–60.

31. See Carol C. Gould, *Rethinking Democracy* (Cambridge, England: Cambridge University Press, 1988); and Michael Walzer, *Spheres of Justice: A Defense of Pluralism and Equality* (New York: Basic Books, 1983).

32. Walzer, *Spheres of Justice*, 301.

33. Gould, *Rethinking Democracy*, 135–43.

34. U.S. Conference of Catholic Bishops, *Economic Justice for All*, 148–49.

35. Two sources to consult for information about the benefits and problems of cooperatives are Robert Jackall and Henry M. Levin, *Worker Cooperatives in America* (Berkeley: University of California, 1984); and William Foote Whyte and Kathleen King Whyte, *Making Mondregon: The Growth and Dynamics of the Worker Cooperative Complex* (Ithaca, N.Y.: ILR Press, 1988).

36. Beverly Wildung Harrison, *Making the Connections: Essays in Feminist Social Ethics*, ed. Carol S. Robb (Boston: Beacon, 1985), 90.

index

Abortion: as component of procreative choice, 129; misplaced concern about, 134; by race, 36; women who obtain, 35–36
Accountability of capital to justice, 144, 147–48
Affirmative Action, 69, 89
Aid to Families with Dependent Children (AFDC), 45
American Civil Liberties Union, 67
American Medical Association, 73
Attachment studies, 42
Authority in ethics: Bible as, 8, 19, 106–7, 156; experience of women as, 147–55; tradition as, 143–47

Bergmann, Barbara, 28
Berns, Walter, 66
Bible: as authority in ethics, 8, 19, 106–7, 156; views of, on economics, 8–18; views of, on homosexuality, 104–7
Bisexuality, 92; policies regarding, 100; sexual ethics for, 119
Bodily self-determination (bodily integrity), 116–17; challenged by disease, 126–28; in sexual ethics, 112, 114, 116–17
Boston Women's Health Book Collective, 113
Bradford, David, 53–54

Centers for Disease Control, 35
Child care: effects on children and families, 38, 41–43; financing for, 39–40, 149; government's responsibility for, 40, 148; high quality of, constituted by, 43; policies supported in other countries, 38–39; and poverty, 44–47; as private matter, 39, 48; and religious organizations, 48–50; responsibility for, 139; as support for battered women, 89; as vocation, 33–34, 43–44
Childbearing: and adoption, 24; benefits and fertility rates, 38; difference in impact on women than men, 35; economic impact of, 24; impact on education, 24–27; income replacement during, 38; and parental leave effect on wages, 32, 140; rates of, 24; of teenage women, 24–26
Child rearing, 31, 33–34
Children: custody battles for gay or lesbian parents of, 108; development of, with gay or lesbian parent, 108–9; as economic actors, 130; effects of substitute child care on, 41–43; Jesus' attitude toward, 14; sexual abuse by adult of, 116; as women's work, 118
"Chivalrous Knight," 53
Civil Rights Act (1964), Section 703 of Title VII, 56, 67, 69, 140
Civil rights of lesbians and gays, 93, 94, 100–101
Cobb, John Jr., 153
Cobbe, Francis Power, 80